Developing Projects Using
C++

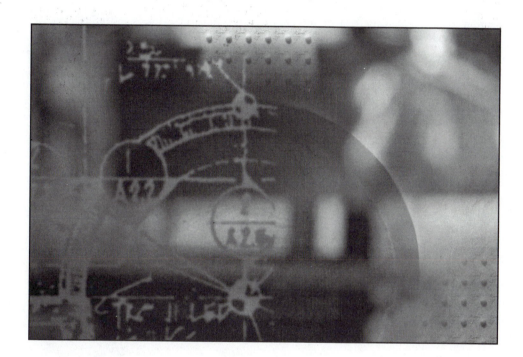

Jo Ann Smith

COURSE TECHNOLOGY

ONE MAIN STREET, CAMBRIDGE, MA 02142

an International Thomson Publishing company I(T)P®

Cambridge • Albany • Bonn • Boston • Cincinnati • London • Madrid • Melbourne • Mexico City
New York • Paris • San Francisco • Singapore • Tokyo • Toronto • Washington

Developing Projects Using C++ is published by Course Technology.

Managing Editor	Kristen Duerr
Product Manager	Cheryl Ouellette
Developmental Editor	Jessica Evans
Associate Production Manager	Seth Andrews
Text Designer	Douglas Goodman
Cover Designer	Efrats Reis

© 1999 by Course Technology— I(T)P®
A division of International Thomson Publishing

For more information contact:

Course Technology
One Main Street
Cambridge, MA 02142

International Thomson Editores
Seneca, 53
Colonia Polanco
11560 Mexico D.F. Mexico

ITP Europe
Berkshire House 168-173
High Holborn
London WCIV 7AA
England

ITP GmbH
Königswinterer Strasse 418
53227 Bonn
Germany

ITP Asia
60 Albert Street, #15-01
Albert Complex
Singapore 189969

Nelson ITP Australia
102 Dodds Street
South Melbourne, 3205
Victoria, Australia

ITP Nelson Canada
1120 Birchmount Road
Scarborough, Ontario
Canada M1K 5G4

ITP Japan
Hirakawacho Kyowa Building, 3F
2-2-1 Hirakawacho
Chiyoda-ku, Tokyo 102
Japan

ISBN 0-7600-5854-7

Printed in the United States of America

2 3 4 5 6 7 8 9 10 MZ 03 02 01 00

Preface

Developing Projects Using C++ is designed to provide students with an opportunity to develop C++ programs that they might encounter in a real-life programming environment. Throughout the book, students practice designing and developing C++ programs, as well as modifying and debugging existing C++ programs. Students also have an opportunity to develop large-scale applications and add functionality to them throughout the term. You can use this book to supplement any introductory C++ programming text. Although this book provides a review of C++ concepts, it assumes that students will learn concepts in more detail and depth from an introductory textbook or from the instructor.

Organization and Coverage

Developing Projects Using C++ contains 10 chapters. Each chapter reviews important concepts that students will have learned in their introductory C++ class. Each section of the chapter contains several exercises from three categories—Modify, Debug, and Develop—that reinforce the section's contents. Four larger-scale projects appear at the end of each chapter. Two of the projects continue throughout the book, allowing students to add functionality or modify the application during the term. Students will complete the two independent, smaller projects while they learn the concepts presented in that chapter.

When students finish with this book, they will have gained extensive practice in developing large- and small-scale programs and in modifying or debugging C++ programs written by another programmer.

Approach

Developing Projects Using C++ distinguishes itself from other C++ books because of its unique approach, which provides students with the opportunity to solve problems that they might encounter as real-life programmers. Much of a programmer's time is spent maintaining existing code either by modifying or debugging programs. Many traditional textbooks include problems where students must develop their own programs from scratch. Students, however, also need practice in reading programs written by other programmers, understanding these programs, and then making modifications that might add functionality, change the methods employed to store data, or correct problems with the code. This book provides that practice.

Another distinguishing characteristic is the incremental approach to program development used in the end-of-chapter Progressive Projects.

This book is written in a modular format and provides exercises after reviewing each major topic. Topics are introduced in an order that is consistent with most introductory C++ textbooks. As a result, instructors and students should find it easy to use this book as a supplement to any primary text. The exercises make excellent lab assignments, and you can use the end-of-chapter projects as programming assignments.

Features

Developing Projects Using C++ includes the following superior features:

- **"Read This Before You Begin" Page** illustrates Course Technology's unequaled commitment to helping instructors introduce technology into the classroom. Technical considerations and assumptions about hardware and software are listed in one place to help instructors save time and eliminate unnecessary aggravation.

- **Exercises** are included for each major section of the book. They focus students on developing new applications; modifying existing programs to add functionality, improve methods of storing data, or reorganize the programs; and debugging existing programs.

- **Examples** are used throughout each chapter to illustrate how to use the C++ programming language.

- A **Summary** at the end of each chapter recaps the programming concepts and commands covered in that chapter.

- Each chapter concludes with two **Progressive Projects** and two **Independent Projects** that deal with contemporary topics. Multiple projects give instructors and students flexibility in their choice of programming challenges.

  - *Progressive Projects*   The two Progressive (continuing) Projects that students develop using the concepts reviewed in the chapter are complete applications. These projects are designed to allow students to develop C++ programs incrementally.

  - *Independent Projects*   The two Independent Projects do not build upon work completed in a previous chapter. Instead, these smaller projects ask students to create smaller applications to solve smaller problems.

Software

This book was written to be compiler-independent. While differences exist in the interfaces used by different compilers, the C++ code itself is standard. All example programs, exercises, and projects were tested using Microsoft Visual C++, version 5.0, and Inprise C++, version 5.0. In a UNIX environment, the only change needed in the C++ code affects the method used to specify a full path-name for a file. (The instructor's CD-ROM contains UNIX student files in the UNIX folder.)

Acknowledgments

I would like to thank all of the people who helped to make this book possible, especially Jessica Evans, my Developmental Editor, who offered me encouragement, patience, humor, and flexibility when I needed it. Her expertise has made this text a better book. Thanks also to Kristen Duerr, Managing Editor, and Cheryl Ouellette, Product Manager, for their patience, support, and flexibility. Thanks also to Seth Andrews, Production Editor; Jill E. Hobbs, Copyeditor; and Brian McCooey and John Bosco, Quality Assurance testers.

I am grateful to the many reviewers who provided helpful and insightful comments during the development of this book, including Albert E. Cawns, Webster University; Richard J. Coppins, Virginia Commonwealth University; Joseph F. Laiacona, Columbia College Chicago; Joan Ramuta, University of St. Francis; Suzanne Sever, Wayne State College; and Jack Thompson, University of Tennessee at Chattanooga.

Finally, I would like to dedicate this book to my family, especially my husband, Ray, and my son, Tim. Your wife, mother, daughter, or sister has returned!

Jo Ann Smith

Contents

Read This Before You Begin

To the Student

Student Disks

To complete the exercises and projects in this book, you need Student Disks. Your instructor will provide you with student files. When you begin each chapter, make sure you are using the correct Student Disk.

Using Your Own Computer

You can use your own computer to complete the exercises and projects in this book. To do so, you will need a C++ compiler. This book was written in such as way that you can use any C++ compiler to complete the exercises and projects. The programs in this book were written and tested using the Microsoft Visual C++, version 5.0 compiler, as well as the Inprise C++, version 5.0 compiler. If you are using Microsoft Visual C++, you must compile your programs from your hard drive, because Visual C++ creates large intermediate files in the compilation process that will not fit on a floppy disk. If you are using the Inprise compiler, however, then all of the exercises and projects for this book will fit on a single high-density floppy disk.

To the Instructor

To complete the chapters in this book, your students must use a set of student files. You must be a registered adopter of this book to receive these files. Follow the instructions in the Help file to copy the student files to your server or stand-alone computer. You can view the Help file using a text editor such as WordPad or Notepad.

Once the files are copied, you can make Student Disks for the students yourself, or tell students where to find the files so they can make their own Student Disks. If your students are using the Microsoft Visual C++, version 5.0 compiler, then they must compile their programs from a hard drive—the student files will not compile correctly on a floppy disk. In this case, students can read data files from drive A. UNIX users should use the student files in the UNIX folder on the instructor's CD-ROM so the files will compile properly.

Course Technology Student Files

You are granted a license to copy the student files to any computer or computer network used by students who have purchased this book.

CHAPTER 1

Programming Overview

Introduction ▶ Chapter 1 assumes that you learned basic programming techniques in either your C++ class or another programming course. This chapter reviews the steps involved in problem solving, provides an overview of procedural programming, and reviews the basic programming constructs.

Steps in Problem Solving for Programming

You should follow six steps to solve programming problems: analyze and understand the problem; develop a general solution; verify your solution; translate your solution into a program using a programming language; verify your program; and make any necessary changes to arrive at the correct output.

Step 1: Analyze and understand the problem. To analyze and understand the problem that you must solve, you must ask questions such as the following:

- What must the program do? For example, does it calculate payroll, draw graphical images, or simulate the arrival and take-off of planes from an airport?
- What data are available for solving the problem?
- In what format are the data stored? For example, you might need to determine the maximum length of a field that stores a person's last name or decide to store Social Security numbers with or without the dashes between groups of numbers.
- Where do the data come from?
- How much data are available?
- Who is responsible for gathering or maintaining the data?
- What result or output should the program produce?
- What should the output look like?

Step 2: Develop a general solution. In a logical order, define the steps needed to solve your problem.

Step 3: Verify your solution. Test your solution by following the steps you outlined in Step 2 by using samples of real data. Can you solve the problem and arrive at the correct result? If not, repeat the previous step until you can solve the problem.

Step 4: Translate your solution into a program. Use the solution that you found in Step 3 and translate it using a programming language, such as C++.

Step 5: Verify your program. Step through the program on paper using examples of real data. Then run the program with similar examples.

Step 6: Make changes as necessary. Repeat Step 5 until you have a working solution.

Example 1-1 shows a programming problem and its solution based on these steps.

Example 1-1

Scout's sporting goods store is having a 25 percent off sale on basketballs, baseballs, and footballs. You need to write a program that allows a clerk to enter the original price of the different types of balls. Your program should use this input to compute the discounted price (that is, the original price minus 25 percent). The output of your program should be the original price and the discounted price on separate lines.

Solution:

Step 1: Analyze and understand the problem. Do you have enough information to solve the problem? The answer to this question is "yes." You could ask the manager for the original prices of the balls, but you really don't need this information because the clerk will enter these prices.

Step 2: Develop a general solution. Your general solution is as follows:

Ask the user to enter the original price.
Get the original price.
Set the discounted price to the original price and multiply it by 0.75 (round up).
Print the original price.
Print the discounted price.

Step 3: Verify your solution. Figure 1-1 shows your general solution and how it works using real data.

General Solution Steps	Example
Ask the user to enter the original price	// User enters 15.95
Get the original price	// Get 15.95
Set the discounted price to the original price and multiply it by 0.75 (round up)	// Discounted price = 15.95 * 0.75 // (round up)
Print the original price	// Original price is 15.95
Print the discounted price	// Discounted price is 11.96
	// The solution works!

Figure 1-1: Verify your solution

Step 4: Translate your solution into a program using a programming language. You will translate your solution later, when you know more about C++.

Step 5: Verify your program. You will verify your program later, when you are more familiar with C++.

Step 6: Make changes as necessary and then repeat Step 5 until you have a working solution. If you experienced syntax errors when compiling your program or if you received incorrect results when running your program, you would make the necessary changes to your C++ program and then repeat Steps 5 and 6 until it works correctly.

Exercises

Exercise 1.1 ▶

You work at a small, family-owned printing business. Your manager asked you to write a program that calculates an employee's weekly net pay according to the following rules: A clerk will enter the employee's name, the number of hours the employee worked (no overtime hours allowed), and the employee's rate of pay. Your program must calculate federal withholding tax (20 percent of gross pay) and Social Security tax (or FICA, representing 8 percent of gross pay). Your program should print the following information on separate lines: the employee's name, gross pay, amount of federal withholding tax, amount of FICA tax, and the employee's net pay. The following solution is correct:

Ask for the employee's name.
Get the employee's name.
Ask for the number of hours worked.
Get the number of hours worked.
Ask for the rate of pay.
Get the rate of pay.
Multiply the number of hours by the rate of pay and assign the result to the gross pay.
Multiply the gross pay by 0.20 and assign this amount to the federal withholding tax.
Multiply the gross pay by 0.08 and assign this amount to FICA.
Subtract the federal withholding tax amount and FICA tax amount from the gross pay and assign the result to the net pay.
Print the employee's name.
Print the employee's gross pay amount.
Print the federal withholding tax amount.
Print the FICA tax amount.
Print the employee's net pay amount.

Now your manager wants you to modify this problem solution. You must define the net pay as the gross pay minus the federal withholding tax, FICA, and state income tax. The state income tax amount is 2 percent of an employee's gross pay. You also need to add the amount of state income tax to the program output. On a piece of paper, change the previous problem solution to include these new requirements.

Exercise 1.2 ▶

You work at a local video rental store. The assistant manager wants you to write a program that calculates the late charges assigned to a customer based on the following rules: Customers rent videos at a rate of $2.00 per day, which is paid when they check out videos. They can keep each video for one day. The store charges a late fee of $1.00 per day when the video is returned past the due date. A clerk will enter the following information when a customer returns the video: customer name, video title, and number of late days (which might be zero days).

Your program should print the following information on separate lines: the customer's name, the name of the video, and the late charge. The following problem solution is incorrect:

Ask for the customer name.
Get the customer name.
Ask for the title of the video.
Get the title of the video.
Ask for the number of late days.
Get the number of late days.
Multiply the number of late days by 2.00 and assign the result to the late charge.
Print the customer name.
Print the title of the video.
Print the late charge.

On a piece of paper, change this incorrect problem solution so that it calculates the rental charge correctly.

Exercise 1.3 ▶

DEVELOP

Follow Steps 1 through 3 of the programming problem-solving process to create a problem solution for the following problem description.

You work at a local garden supply store. Your manager has asked you to write a program that calculates the number of bags of fertilizer needed to cover a lawn. A clerk will enter the dimensions of the lawn (length and width) in feet. A 20-pound bag of fertilizer can cover a lawn area as large as 5,000 square feet. Your program should print the lawn's dimensions and the number of bags of fertilizer needed to ensure proper coverage on separate lines. If the answer is a fractional number, the program should round it up. For example, if the customer needs 1.4 bags of fertilizer to ensure proper coverage, your program should output that the customer must buy 2 bags of fertilizer.

Procedural Programming Overview

After you define and understand a problem, it might be too large to write as one long program. In such a case, you should break the large problem into a group of smaller problems. Then you can create the smaller pieces, or modules, and give them a simple interface. An **interface** refers to the way that a module will be used in the program, such as what information the program will pass into the module and what output the module will produce.

To use a module, a programmer should understand what it does (its function), what it needs to accomplish its work (data passed in), and what the results are (its outputs). At this stage of the programming process, do not worry about how the module will actually solve the problem. Example 1-2 shows how to use a module.

Example 1-2

C++ provides a library function named sqrt() that calculates the square root of a number. This square root function expects a number to be passed to it and then produces the square root of the number as its output. You do not have to understand how this function calculates the square root. Instead, you can think of it as a black box that can be diagrammed as shown in Figure 1-2.

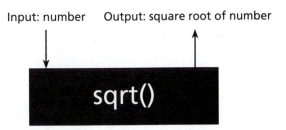

Figure 1-2: Square root function—a black box

After you collect the information needed to understand a problem, you can use structure charts to design the program in terms of modules/black boxes. For example, Figure 1-3 is a structure chart of the process of making lasagna.

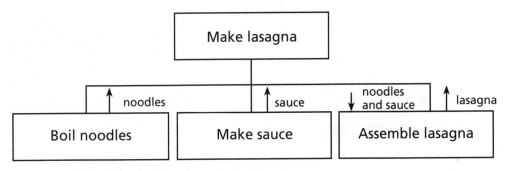

Figure 1-3: Structure chart for making lasagna

If the modules are still too big, you can break the modules into subordinate modules, like those shown in Figure 1-4.

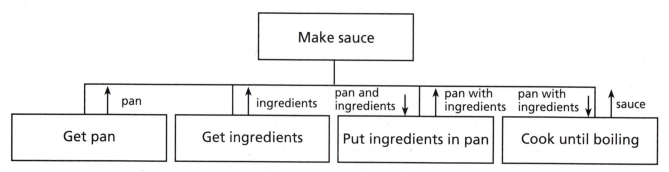

Figure 1-4: Structure chart for making sauce

Continue creating modules and submodules until the solution is fully specified.

Exercises

Exercise 1.4 ▶

MODIFY

The structure chart for making lasagna shown in Figure 1-3 is incomplete. On a piece of paper, add any submodules that are needed for the Boil Noodles module.

Exercise 1.5 ▶

DEBUG

Decomposing a problem into its smaller problems is not always done correctly. Below are some examples that you might encounter every day. On a piece of paper, describe what is wrong with these problem solutions.

On the back of your shampoo bottle: Step 1: Lather; Step 2: Rinse; Step 3: Repeat.

On the inside lid of the washing machine at the laundromat: Step 1: Load clothes loosely; Step 2: Add detergent before loading clothes; Step 3: Insert quarters; Step 4: Start machine.

Exercise 1.6 ▶

DEVELOP

On a piece of paper, create a structure chart for the following problem. Make sure that you specify the solution in enough detail. How do you make a pot of coffee? Assume that you are using a drip-type coffee maker.

Programming Constructs Overview

Programs consist of programming constructs. Programmers use combinations of programming constructs, such as data manipulation statements and control structures, to write programs. The statements in this section are written in pseudocode rather than in C++.

Data manipulation statements are statements that perform calculations, such as `number1 * 10;`, or that copy information from one place in memory to another, such as `number1 = number2;`. Such statements also might get input, such as `get value of number1 from user;` or provide output, such as `print value of number1;`.

Control structures are statements that specify the order in which to execute statements. Simple sequence statements, unless instructed otherwise, are executed sequentially, one after the other. For example, the following statements are simple statements:

Get value of number1
Multiply number1 by 10
Print value of number1

Repetition is the process by which you repeat a statement or a group of statements over and over. Repetition usually is referred to as a **loop**. C++ includes the following repetition statements: while, do while, and for. All loops contain two parts—the statement or statements to be repeated, and a condition used to determine when the repetition should stop. The **while loop** will execute zero or more times, depending on whether some condition is true or false. For example, the following while loop executes while the number is less than 10:

```
number = 5
while (number is less than 10)
     print number
     add 1 to number
end of while loop
```

The following **do while** loop will execute one or more times, depending on whether some condition is true or false:

```
number = 5
do
     print number
     add 1 to number
while (number is less than 10)
```

The **for loop** is a good choice if you know how many times a loop should execute. For example, the following for loop executes exactly 25 times:

```
max_students = 25
for (num = 1; while num is less than or equal to max_students; add 1 to num)
     get grade for a student
     print grade for a student
end of for loop
```

Selection means that a statement or a group of statements will be executed depending on whether a specific condition is true or false. C++ has the following selection statements: if, if else, and switch. The **if statement** is a single-path selection statement:

```
if (value of number is 1)
     print "Number is 1"
```

The **if else** statement is a dual-path selection statement:

```
if (value of number is 1)
     print "Number is 1"
else
     print "Number is NOT 1"
```

The following pseudocode illustrates how to nest if statements to create a multi-path selection statement:

```
if (value of number is 1)
     print "Value of number is 1"
else if (value of number is 2)
     print "Value of number is 2"
else
     print "Value of number is NOT 1 or 2"
```

The **switch** statement is also a multipath selection statement:

```
switch (number)
begin switch
     case 1:        print "Value of number is 1"
     case 2:        print "Value of number is 2"
     case default:  print "Value of number is NOT 1 or 2"
end switch
```

Invocation takes place when one routine calls another routine by name. Program control passes to the named routine along with input values, the routine performs its work, and then control returns to the point of invocation. For example:

```
Begin program
    Prompt user for input
    Get input and store it in number
    Invoke square_root function (pass the value of number)
    Assign output of square_root function to result
    Print the value of result
End program
Begin routine square_root (input value)
    Calculate the square root of the input value
    Return result
End routine square_root
```

You can include or **nest** any of these control structures within one another. For example, you can have an `if` statement and several sequential statements within the same loop.

Exercises

Exercise 1.7 ▶ What type of manipulation statement, control structure, or combination of manipulation statements and control structures would you choose to accomplish the following tasks? Write your answers on a piece of paper.

  a. The user of your program will input an employee's salary.
  b. You need to calculate the salaries for 25 employees. Salaries for all employees are calculated in the same way.
  c. An employee's salary is calculated differently if he or she has worked overtime hours (that is, if the number of hours worked in a single week is greater than 40).
  d. Discounts are calculated differently based on the quantity purchased. The discount is 5 percent if 5 or fewer items are purchased, 10 percent if 6 to 10 items are purchased, 15 percent if 11 to 15 items are purchased, and 20 percent if more than 15 items are purchased.
  e. The value stored in `number1` is 10. You need to make a copy of the value stored in `number1` and place the copy in `number2`.
  f. You need to print the value stored in `number1`.
  g. You need to get three values from a user of your program and then print them on the user's screen.
  h. You need to calculate the gross pay for 25 employees. The gross pay will be calculated differently if the employee has worked overtime hours (more than 40 hours worked in a single week). You also need to print the number of hours worked and the salary for each employee.

Exercise 1.8 ▶

D E V E L O P

On a piece of paper, solve the following problem by using manipulation statements and control structures. Write a program that calculates an employee's weekly net pay according to the following rules. A clerk will enter the employee's name, number of hours worked, and rate of pay. Your program will calculate the gross pay for working 40 or fewer hours in a single week, the gross pay for working overtime hours (hours worked in excess of 40 in a single week at a pay rate equaling the regular pay rate plus 50 percent of this pay rate), the federal withholding tax amount (20 percent of the total gross pay amount), the Social Security tax (FICA) amount (8 percent of the total gross pay amount), and the state income tax amount (2 percent of the total gross pay amount).

Your program should print the following information on separate lines: employee's name, employee's gross pay, amount of federal withholding tax, amount of FICA tax, amount of state income tax, and employee's net pay amount.

S U M M A R Y

- To design good solutions to problems, use the six steps for problem solving.

- To design procedural programs, break a large problem into a group of smaller problems, called modules.

- Modules should have a simple interface that identifies what to pass to the module and what is returned from the module.

- Programs consist of constructs such as data manipulation statements and control structures.

- Data manipulation statements perform calculations, copy information, get input, or provide output.

- Control structures specify the order in which statements should be executed. The different types of control structures include simple sequence statements, repetition statements, selection statements, and invocation statements.

P R O G R E S S I V E   P R O J E C T S

You will complete one or both of the progressive projects as you work through this book by adding functionality in each of the projects throughout the term. Eventually, you will use C++ to complete the project. For this chapter, you should read the project descriptions. Remember that the progressive projects are large problems that you need to decompose into smaller problems. Use a structure chart to help with the decomposition. After completing your structure chart, choose one of the submodules and use appropriate data manipulation statements and flow of control statements to solve the smaller problem identified in this submodule. Keep in mind that you are new to this type of problem solving, so your first attempt at design will not necessarily be your last.

1. Books and More

Bill Reading, the owner of a local bookstore named Books and More, wants to automate his inventory control system. Bill hired you to create the system. You have had several meetings with him to determine the functions that the system will provide for the bookstore. You identified the following functions:

- The system must remain online while the bookstore is open. When the bookstore opens in the morning, the inventory will be read into your program from the inventory file, inBooks.dat. When the bookstore closes for the day, the updated inventory should be saved to the same file.
- When the bookstore receives shipments, the inventory must be updated either by adding to the number in stock or by adding a new entry if the book is not currently present in the inventory.
- When books go out of print, the inventory should be updated by deleting the entry, but only when stock levels fall to zero.
- Each time a book is sold, the inventory must be updated.
- Bill wants to be able to get a complete listing of the inventory, listed alphabetically by the book title.
- He also wants to be able to list the complete bibliographical information for a particular book.
- The program must generate a list of the titles of all books in the inventory and indicate how many copies of each book were sold each day.

Through your meetings, you also determined the information that must be maintained for each book in the inventory. The following information will be stored in the inBooks.dat inventory file for each book:

■ title (50 characters maximum)
■ author's last name (30 characters maximum)
■ author's first name (20 characters maximum)
■ price
■ publisher (30 characters maximum)
■ ISBN
■ copyright date
■ quantity on hand
■ status (1 for an in-print book or 0 for an out-of-print book)

2. Baseball Simulation

Programmers write computer programs to simulate some other operation, such as that of an airplane, an automobile, a VCR, or a game such as baseball. In this project, you will write a simulation of a baseball game. The baseball simulation has the following elements:

■ An announcer will introduce the two teams and their starting lineups. The announcer will give the score at the end of each half-inning, along with the inning number. For example, an announcer might say "In the bottom of the fifth inning, the score is the Chicago White Sox 5 and the Detroit Tigers 3."
■ Pitchers will throw curveballs, fastballs, sinkers, and sliders.
■ Three outfielders will play in right, center, and left field.
■ Four infielders will play shortstop and first, second, and third base.
■ There is a single catcher.
■ Batters can take as many as four balls or three strikes as thrown by the pitcher. They can hit a single, double, triple, or homerun.
■ The two teams will play for nine innings and your simulation will keep score. At the end of the game, the announcer will announce the final score.

INDEPENDENT PROJECTS

1. Making a Telephone Call

Use a structure chart to decompose the steps you take to make a telephone call into smaller problems. After creating this structure chart, use appropriate data manipulation statements and flow of control statements to specify solutions to the smaller problems.

2. Calculator

Use a structure chart to decompose the following problem into smaller problems. You need to write a program that functions as a calculator. Your calculator should be able to add two numbers, subtract two numbers, multiply two numbers, or divide two numbers. It should allow a user to continue adding, subtracting, multiplying, or dividing numbers until the user decides to quit the program. The user can enter two different numbers each time the program runs. After creating a structure chart, use appropriate data manipulation statements and flow of control statements to solve the smaller problems.

Variables, Data Types, Operators, and Input/Output

Introduction ▶ In Chapter 1, you reviewed the basics of problem solving and programming. In this chapter, you will review the basics of C++ programming, which include declaring and using variables and constants, using the built-in data types, inserting comments, working with C++ operators, writing and using expressions, and understanding simple input and output in C++.

C++ Programs

Files that contain C++ programs are named using the .cpp file extension (for example, hello.cpp). All C++ programs must have a `main()` function to indicate where the program execution begins. The `main()` function, as well as all other functions in a C++ program, begins with an opening curly brace and ends with a closing curly brace ({ and }). The `main()` function usually is written to return an integer value—though this format is a convention, and not a rule, adopted by C++ programmers. C++ is case-sensitive—the compiler knows the difference between uppercase and lowercase letters. For example, it sees *text* and *Text* as different variables. The statement `#include <iostream.h>` is a preprocessor directive that is included in a C++ program to allow the program to perform input and output. You will learn about preprocessor directives in Chapter 9. The C++ program shown in Example 2-1 is stored in a file named Ex2-1.cpp in the Examples folder in the Chapter2 folder on your Student Disk. This C++ program prints the word "Hello" on the screen.

Example 2-1

```
// Ex2-1.cpp
// This program prints the word "Hello" on the screen.
#include <iostream.h> // Preprocessor directive
// This function returns an integer.
// Execution begins here.
int main()
{   // C++ functions begin with {
    // C++ statement that prints "Hello" on the screen
    cout << "Hello." << endl;
    return 0;    // This function returns an integer.
}   // C++ functions end with }
```

Exercise

Exercise 2.1 ▶ Find and correct the errors in the following C++ program.

D E B U G

```
// welcome.cpp
// This program prints "Welcome to the C++ course."
// on the screen.

begin ()

    cout << "Welcome to the C++ course." << endl;

}
```

Identifiers and Variables

An **identifier** is a named memory location. A **variable** is an identifier that C++ programs use to store values needed by your program. Variable names in C++ can consist of letters, numerical digits, and the underscore character, but they *cannot begin* with a digit. In ANSI C++, the lengths of variable names are not limited.

You should give your variables meaningful names. When naming variables, remember that you cannot use a C++ keyword. A **keyword** is a word that the compiler reserves with a special meaning. See Appendix A for a list of C++ keywords.

Exercise

Exercise 2.2 ▶ Is each of the following a legal C++ variable name? Answer yes or no.

_____	my_var	_____	num6
_____	your_var	_____	float
_____	friend	_____	VALUE
_____	5May	_____	vlaue
_____	i_am_a_variable	_____	Value
_____	value	_____	intValue

Data Types

You must declare all C++ variables and specify a particular data type before you can use them. A variable's **data type** dictates the amount of memory that is allocated and the range of values that you can store at that memory location. Figure 2-1 lists the four basic C++ data types.

Data Type	Size	Value Range
char	8 bits (1 byte)	-128 to 127

int	Size of an integer, which is the same as the word size of the computer:
	  16-bit word size (2 bytes)
	  32-bit word size (4 bytes)
		
		-32,768 to 32,767
		-2,147,483,648 to 2,147,483,647

float	32 bits (4 bytes)	3.4×10^{-38} to $3.4 \times 10^{+38}$
double	64 bits (8 bytes)	1.7×10^{-308} to $1.7 \times 10^{+308}$

Figure 2-1: Basic C++ data types

The qualifiers you can use in C++ are long, short, or unsigned, as illustrated in Figure 2-2. You use the qualifier **unsigned** with data types char and int. You can store only positive values in an unsigned char or unsigned int. You use the qualifier **long** with data types int and double. You use the qualifier **short** with data type int. Notice that a long int is 32 bits in size and a short int is 16 bits in size, regardless of the word size of the computer. Using short ints and long ints rather than ints in your C++ programs provides portability for your C++ programs. **Portability** means that you can move your C++ programs from one computer to another, and the programs will work correctly without any changes to the code.

Data Type	Size	Value Range
unsigned char	8 bits (1 byte)	0 to 255
unsigned short int	16 bits (2 bytes)	0 to 65,536
unsigned long int	32 bits (4 bytes)	0 to 4,294,967,296
short int	16 bits (2 bytes)	-32,768 to 32,767
long int	32 bits (4 bytes)	-2,147,483,648 to 2,147,483,647
long double	80 bits (10 bytes)	3.4×10^{-4932} to $1.1 \times 10^{+4932}$

Figure 2-2: C++ qualifiers

Exercise

Exercise 2.3 ▶ What data type is appropriate to store the following values?

a. _____ A person's age

b. _____ The first letter of a person's last name

c. _____ The amount of a discount, such as 15 percent

d. _____ The distance between Chicago and Detroit

e. _____ The price of a birthday gift

Syntax
· · · · · · · · · · · · · · · · ·
▶ data_type variable_name;

Declaring C++ Variables

You must declare all C++ variables before you can use them. For example, `short int counter;` declares a variable named `counter` with a short int data type. By default, the variable is signed if the declaration does not specify that it is unsigned. The compiler reserves 16 bits (2 bytes) of memory for the variable named `counter`, and the name `counter` now is associated with a memory address, as shown in Figure 2-3.

counter (Variable name)

```
┌─────────────────────────┐
│                         │
└─────────────────────────┘
```

1000 (Memory address assigned by compiler and associated with the variable named counter)

Figure 2-3: Declaration of variable and memory allocation

You can initialize a C++ variable when you declare it. When you initialize a C++ variable, you give it an initial value. For example, you can assign an initial value of zero to the `counter` variable when you declare it using the following statement: `short int counter = 0;`. Figure 2-4 shows the initialized `counter` variable.

counter (Variable name)

```
┌─────────────────────────┐
│                        0│ ──────────────▶  Initialized with 0
└─────────────────────────┘
```

1000 (Memory address assigned by compiler and associated with the variable named counter)

Figure 2-4: Initialization of variable and memory allocation

Exercise

Exercise 2.4 ▶ Write a declaration for each of the following variables.

a. _____ Declare a variable to store a student's numeric test score (0 to 100).

b. _____ Declare a variable to store a student's letter grade test score (A, B, C, D, or F).

c. _____ Declare a variable to store the first initial of a person's first name.

d. _____ Declare a variable to store the number of students in a class.

e. _____ Declare and initialize a variable to store today's high temperature.

f. _____ Declare a variable to store the price of an item.

C++ Constants

Integer constants can be represented as decimal (base 10), octal (base 8), or hexadecimal (base 16) integers. Figure 2-5 shows how integer constants are used.

Integer Constant Interpreted as	Value	Example
Decimal (base 10)	25	x = 25;
Octal (base 8)	025 (leading 0)	x = 025;
Hexadecimal (base 16)	0x25 (leading 0x or 0X)	x = 0x25;
Long	25L (trailing L or l)	x = 25L;
Unsigned	25U (trailing U or u)	x = 25U;

Figure 2-5: Using integer constants

Floating-point constants are of data type double. Figure 2-6 shows examples of floating-point constants.

Floating Point Constant Interpreted as	Value	Example
Double	3.14	num = 3.14;
Scientific notation (double)	3.14 e–2	num = 3.14 e-2;
float	3.14F (trailing F or f)	num = 3.14F;

Figure 2-6: Using floating-point constants

Character constants are represented by a numeric value corresponding to the ASCII character set. (Appendix B lists ASCII characters and their numeric values expressed as decimal, binary, and hexadecimal integers.) You must enclose character constants in single quotation marks when using them in a C++ statement. Character constants have a size equal to the size of an integer. Figure 2-7 shows examples of character constants.

Character Constant	Description	ASCII Value	Example
'a'	Character a	97	ch = 'a'; or ch = 97;
'5'	Character 5	53	ch = '5'; or ch = 53;
';'	Character ;	59	ch = ';'; or ch = 59;

Figure 2-7: Using character constants

Figure 2-8 shows some of the special characters available in C++.

Character Constant	Description	ASCII Value	Example
'\n'	New line character	10	ch = '\n';
'\t'	Tab character	9	ch = '\t';
'\a'	Alarm/bell character	7	ch = '\a';
'\0'	Null character	0	ch = '\0';

Figure 2-8: Special C++ characters

A **string constant** consists of a series of zero or more characters enclosed in double quotation marks. C++ places a null character ('\0') at the end of a constant string.

You declare a **constant** variable by using the `const` attribute. The **const attribute** specifies a C++ variable that should have a constant value. Constant variables must be initialized, and you cannot change the value of a constant variable. In this book, constant variables appear in all uppercase letters. An example of a constant variable is PI, which is declared as `const double PI = 3.14159;`.

Syntax
....
▶ const data_type var_name;

Exercise

Exercise 2.5 ▶ Declare and initialize constant variables with the following values.

a. _____ Initialize a constant variable with the value of PI (3.14159).

b. _____ Initialize a constant variable of data type double with the value 1.2.

c. _____ Initialize a constant variable of data type float with the value 1.2.

d. _____ Initialize a constant variable with the hexadecimal value FF.

e. _____ Initialize a constant variable with the newline character.

C++ Comments

You include **comments** in a C++ program to improve the program's readability. The compiler ignores comments, allowing the programmer to insert text that describes the program, a specific statement in the program, or a group of statements without affecting how the program works. Two commenting styles are available in C++.

You can type the // characters at the beginning of each comment line or you can enclose a block of text within the characters /* and */. The block comment markers are useful when your comment will span several lines. You can place comments anywhere in a C++ program. Example 2-2 illustrates several placements for both styles of comments.

Example 2-2

```
// Ex2-2.cpp
// Written by Jo Ann Smith
// October 23, 1999

/* This program prints one line to
    the computer screen. */
#include <iostream.h>
int main()
{
  cout << "Hello." << endl;
  return 0;
}
```

Output: Hello.

C++ Operators

Figure 2-9 lists some common C++ operators and their functions.

Operator Name	Operator Symbol	Example	Comment
Addition	+	num1 + num2	
Subtraction	-	value - 50	
Multiplication	*	price * 2	
Division	/	15 / 2	Integer division; result is 7; fraction is truncated.
		15.0 / 2.0	Floating-point division; result is 7.500000.
		15.0 / 2	Floating-point division; result is 7.500000.
Modulus	%	hours % 24	Performs division and finds the remainder; result is 1 if the value of hours is 25; cannot be used with floats or doubles.
Unary minus	-	-(num1 + num2)	If value of (num1 + num2) is 10, then -(num1 + num2) is -10.

Figure 2-9: Common C++ operators

Operator Name	Operator Symbol	Example	Comment
Assignment or initialization	=	count = 5;	Assignment—places the value on the right side into the memory location named on the left side.
		int count = 5;	Initialization—places the value on the right side into the memory location named on the left side when the variable is declared.
Assignment	+=	num += 20;	Equivalent to num = num + 20;
	-=	num -= 15;	Equivalent to num = num - 15;
	*=	num *= 2;	Equivalent to num = num * 2;
	/=	num /= 2;	Equivalent to num = num / 2;
	%=	num %= 5;	Equivalent to num = num % 5;
Parentheses	()	num1 + (num2 * num3)	Controls precedence

Figure 2-9: Common C++ operators (continued)

Precedence refers to the order in which the compiler will execute the operations. Operators have different precedences associated with them. Operators also have **associativity**, which refers to the order in which the compiler will execute operations that have the same precedence. For example, the expression `num1 + num2 - num3` includes two operators that have the same precedence—the addition and the subtraction operator. The two operators have left to right associativity, so the compiler will begin with the leftmost operator and then move to the right. In this case, the subtraction operator will follow the addition operator. Figure 2-10 shows the precedence and associativity of the operators discussed in this chapter.

Operator Name	Operator Symbol(s)	Order of Precedence	Associativity
Parentheses	( )	First	Left to right
Unary	-	Second	Right to left
Multiplication, division, and modulus	* / %	Third	Left to right
Addition and subtraction	+ -	Fourth	Left to right
Assignment	= += -= *= /= %=	Fifth	Right to left

Figure 2-10: Order of precedence

Example 2-3 shows a program that demonstrates operator precedence.

Example 2-3

```cpp
// Ex2-3.cpp
// This program shows the precedence of operators.
#include <iostream.h>
int main()
{
  short int num1 = 5;
  short int num2 = 2;
  short int num3 = 7;
  short int result;

  result = num1 * num2 + num3;
  // The value of result is 17.
  cout << "Value of result is "  << result << "." << endl;
  result = num1 * (num2 + num3);
  // The value of result is 45.
  cout << "Value of result is " << result << "." << endl;

  return 0;
}
```

C++ Expressions

An **expression** combines variables, constants, and operators. The evaluation of an expression results in a value. In a similar fashion, variables evaluate to values, such as value, total, and sum. Constants also evaluate to values, such as 5, 1.5, 'a', and "hello." You can combine variables and constants with operators in expressions, such as num1 + num2 * num3. You also can enclose expressions in parentheses to control the precedence of operations. For example, the expression (num1 + num2) * num3 produces a different output than the expression num1 + num2 * num3 because the operators have a different order of precedence.

C++ Statements

A C++ **statement** specifies an action to be carried out by the computer. Simple statements in C++ must end with a semicolon. Example 2-4 shows a program that uses statements.

Example 2-4

```cpp
// Ex2-4.cpp
// This program illustrates the use of statements.

#include <iostream.h>
int main()
{
  unsigned int counter = 10;
  int num;

  num = 10;
  num *= 5;
```

```
    counter = counter + 6;

    return 0;
}
```

Exercises

Exercise 2.6 ▶

D E V E L O P

On a piece of paper, write a C++ program that converts the temperature of 86 degrees Fahrenheit to its Celsius equivalent. The formula for converting a temperature from Fahrenheit to Celsius is Celsius = (5/9) (Fahrenheit - 32).

Exercise 2.7 ▶

D E V E L O P

On a piece of paper, write a C++ program that computes the circumference of a circle with a radius of 15. The formula to find the circumference of a circle is 2 * PI * r. The value of PI is 3.14160 and the value of r is the radius of the circle.

Exercise 2.8 ▶

D E V E L O P

On a piece of paper, write a C++ program that computes your age on your birthday in the year 2010. Assign appropriate values for your age and the current year.

C++ Input/Output Basics

C++ compilers come with an input/output library. This library contains routines that allow you to perform input and output in your program. In C++, this library is called the **Stream I/O library**. To use the routines in the Stream I/O library, you must add the statement #include <iostream.h> at the beginning of your C++ program. This statement will allow you to perform read and write operations.

Syntax
· · · · · · · · · · · · · ·
▶ output_stream << expression;

The C++ Insertion Operator (<<)

You use the C++ **insertion operator** (<<) to insert data into an output stream. You can use the cout and cerr output streams: **cout** is the standard output stream, which usually is the screen; **cerr** is the standard error stream, which usually is the screen. The insertion operator converts integers, floats, chars, strings, and other values to the appropriate format for display on the screen. For example, cout << intvar; will display the integer stored in the variable named intvar on the screen. You can use the insertion operator repeatedly in a C++ statement without repeating the name of the output stream. For example, cout << floatvar << stringvar; will display the value stored in floatvar followed by the value stored in stringvar. Example 2-5 shows a program that prints values to the screen.

Example 2-5

```
// Ex2-5.cpp
// This program prints values to the screen.

#include <iostream.h>
int main()
{
    int num1 = 10;

    cout << "Hello, world!" << '\n';
```

```
   cout << "The value of num1 is " << num1 << '.' << '\n';

   return 0;
}
```

Output:
```
Hello, world!
The value of num1 is 10.
```

You use **manipulators** with the insertion operator to format the data to be displayed. Figure 2-11 lists two such manipulators and their descriptions.

Manipulator	Description	Example
endl	Causes a newline to be inserted into the output stream; equivalent to using the '\n' character.	cout << "Value of num1 is " << num1\ << '.' << endl;
setw()	Allows you to specify a field width to be occupied by a value. The width is specified as an argument passed to setw(). For example, setw(8) sets the width of the field to eight characters. The next value in the output stream will be printed in a field that is eight characters in length.	cout << setw(8) << num1;

Figure 2-11: Some C++ manipulators

To use most manipulators in your C++ programs, you must add the following line to the beginning of your program: #include <iomanip.h>. The endl manipulator is an exception that may be used without this statement. Example 2-6 shows how to use C++ manipulators in a program.

Example 2-6

```
// Ex2-6.cpp
// This program illustrates the use of manipulators in C++.

#include <iostream.h>
#include <iomanip.h>

int main()
{
  short int num1 = 5, num2 = 10, result;
```

```
    result = num1 + num2;
    cout << "Output" << endl;
    // The \ is used to allow C++ statements
    // to span several lines .
    cout << setw(12) << "Operand1" << setw(5) << '+' \
    << setw(12) << "Operand2" << setw(5) << "is" \
    << setw(8) << result << '.' << endl;
    cout << setw(12) << num1 << setw(5) << '+' \
    << setw(12) << num2 << setw(5) << "is"\
    << setw(8) << result << '.' << endl;

    return 0;
}
```

Output:
```
Operand1     +     Operand2   is     15.
         5   +           10   is     15.
```

Syntax

▶ output_stream.put(ch);

You can use the **put(ch) output function** with an output stream, such as cout and cerr. This function will insert the character stored in the variable named ch into the output stream. Example 2-7 shows a program that uses the put(ch) function.

Example 2-7

```
// Ex2-7.cpp
// This C++ program uses the put(ch) function.

#include <iostream.h>
int main()
{
  char ch1, ch2;
  ch1 = '5';
  ch2 = '.';

  cout.put(ch1);
  cout.put(ch2);
  cout.put(ch1);

  return 0;
}
```

Output: 5.5

Exercises

Exercise 2.9 ▶

MODIFY

In Exercise 2-6, you wrote a C++ program that converted a Fahrenheit temperature to its Celsius equivalent. On a piece of paper, modify the program by adding output statements that print the following information on different lines: The Fahrenheit temperature is <value of Fahrenheit temperature>. The Celsius temperature is <value of Celsius temperature>.

Exercise 2.10 ▶

MODIFY

In Exercise 2-7, you wrote a C++ program that computed the circumference of a circle. On a piece of paper, modify the program by adding output statements that print the following information on different lines: The radius is <value of radius>. The circumference is <value of circumference>.

Exercise 2.11 ▶

In Exercise 2-8, you wrote a C++ program that computed your age in the year 2010. On a piece of paper, modify the program by adding output statements to print the following information on separate lines: You are now <value of age> years old. In the year 2010 you will be <value of age> years old.

Syntax
· · · · · · · · · · · · · · ·

▶ input_stream >> var_name;

The C++ Extraction Operator (>>)

You use the C++ **extraction operator** (>>) to extract data from an input stream, such as `cin`. `cin` is the standard input stream, which usually is the keyboard. The C++ extraction operator converts input typed at the keyboard to the appropriate data type. The whitespace characters space, tab, and newline serve as delimiters to this stream. The user must press the Enter key before data becomes available to your program. Note that the whitespace characters are not extracted from the input stream; they merely stop the input operation. In addition, any leading whitespace characters are skipped and extracted from the input stream before a read operation begins. A whitespace character will never be read and stored in a variable using the extraction operator. Instead, you must use the `get()` function to carry out this operation. For example, `cin >> intvar;` will read from the input stream and skip any leading whitespace characters; it will then read all data in the stream up to a whitespace character. The data read will be stored as an integer if `intvar` is an integer variable.

You can use the extraction operator repeatedly in a C++ statement without repeating the name of the input stream. For example, `cin >> floatvar >> intvar;` will read and store a float in the `floatvar` variable and then read and store an integer in the `intvar` variable. Example 2-8 shows a program that uses the extraction operator.

Example 2-8

```cpp
// Ex2-8.cpp
// This C++ program uses the extraction operator.

#include <iostream.h>
int main()
{
  int id_num;
  char acct_type;
  float payment;
  // Prompt user for input.
  cout << "Please enter your ID number: ";
  // Get user's input.
  cin >> id_num;
  cout << "Please enter your account type: ";
  cin >> acct_type;
  cout << "Please enter the amount of your payment: ";
  cin >> payment;
  // Display data.
  cout << "Your ID number is: " << id_num << endl;
  cout << "Your account type is: " << acct_type << endl;
  cout << "Your monthly payment is: " << payment << endl;

  return 0;
}
```

Input:
```
Please enter your ID number: 1234
Please enter your account type: C
Please enter the amount of your payment: 12.50
```

Output:
```
Your ID number is: 1234
Your account type is: C
Your monthly payment is: 12.5
```

Syntax

▶ input_stream.get(ch);

You use the **get(ch) function** to get a single character from the input stream. The get(ch) function does not ignore whitespace characters. It expects one argument of data type char, which is the name of a variable previously declared in your C++ program. The character extracted from the input stream will be placed in that variable. Example 2-9 shows a program that uses the get(ch) function.

Example 2-9

```cpp
// Ex2-9.cpp
// This program reads a character from the standard
// input stream and echoes the value back to the user.

#include <iostream.h>
int main()
{
  char ch;
  cout << "Enter a character." << endl;
  cin.get(ch);
  cout << "The character you entered is " << ch << endl;
  cin.get(ch);
  // This statement should print a newline character.
  cout << "The character you entered is " << ch << endl;

  return 0;
}
```

Input:
```
Please enter a character: !
```

Output:
```
The character you entered is !
The character you entered is
```

Syntax

▶ input_stream.ignore();

You can use the **ignore() function** to discard characters in the input stream. In the statement cin.ignore(100,'\n');, the first argument is an integer (number of characters) and the second argument is a delimiter character. The arguments instruct the ignore() function to read and discard up to 100 characters from the input stream or to read and discard characters until a newline character is read, whichever comes first. You might use this function, for example, to extract whitespace from the input stream left behind by the extraction operator. You also might use it when the input stream is in an error state and you need to discard the characters that caused the error state to be set.

Syntax

▶ input_stream.clear();

You use the **clear() function** to clear an error condition associated with an input stream. For instance, if your C++ program uses the extraction operator to get user input, the input stream might enter an error state. For example, if your program expects the user to input a salary, your program will expect the user to type in a floating-point number. If the user enters alphabetic characters, the extraction operator will have difficulty reading the input and converting it to a floating-point number. As a result, the input stream will be in an error state. This error state must be cleared before input can begin again. Example 2-10 shows a C++ program that uses the clear() and ignore() functions.

Example 2-10

```
// Ex2-10.cpp
// This program uses the clear() and ignore() functions.

#include <iostream.h>
int main()
{
  double salary;

  cout << "Enter your salary: ";
  cin >> salary;

  // cin is True if it is not in an error state.
  // cin is False if it is in an error state.
  // The if statement is explained in Chapter 4.
  if(!cin)
  {
    cin.clear(); // Clears the error state.
    // Gets rid of unwanted characters.
    cin.ignore(256,'\n');
    cout << "Bad input" << endl;
  }
  else
    cout << "Your salary is " << salary << "." << endl;

  return 0;

}
```

Exercises

Exercise 2.12 ▶

In Exercise 2-9, you wrote a C++ program that converted a Fahrenheit temperature to its Celsius equivalent. Modify the program to get the Fahrenheit temperature from the user of the program. Provide output statements that print the following information on separate lines: The Fahrenheit temperature is <value of Fahrenheit temperature>. The Celsius temperature is <value of Celsius temperature>. Save your program in a file named Ch2-12a.cpp in the Chapter2 folder on your Student Disk. Compile and execute the program.

Exercise 2.13 ▶

D E B U G

The C++ program stored in the file named Ch2-13.cpp in the Chapter2 folder on your Student Disk is supposed to compute the circumference of a circle with a radius that is *provided by the user*. The program also is supposed to print the following information on separate lines: The radius is <value of radius>. The circumference is <value of circumference>. The program does not compile correctly, so you have no way of knowing whether it runs correctly.

Find and fix the errors so that this program will run correctly. Save the corrected program as Ch2-13a.cpp in the Chapter2 folder on your Student Disk.

Exercise 2.14 ▶

Write a C++ program that will allow you to calculate the amount of fencing you need to enclose your backyard. Your program should prompt you to enter the length and width of your backyard in feet and then compute the perimeter. The output of your program should be the calculated perimeter, which is the amount of fencing needed to enclose your backyard. Save your program as Ch2-14a.cpp in the Chapter2 folder on your Student Disk.

File Input/Output in C++

C++ programs can read their input from a file and write their output to a file. To use file I/O in C++ you must:

1. Enter `#include <fstream.h>` at the beginning of your program.
2. Declare a file stream variable—for example, `ifstream in_data;`, where ifstream is the data type for input files, or `ofstream out_data;`, where ofstream is the data type for output files.
3. Open the input and/or output files using the `open()` function and specify the name of the file to open. For example:

   ```
   in_data.open("inStu.dat");
   out_data.open("outStu.dat");
   ```
4. Use the data stored in the input file or write data to the output file.
5. Close the input and/or output files using the `close()` function and specify the name of the file to close. For example:

   ```
   in_data.close();
   out_data.close();
   ```

The File Insertion Operator (<<)

After you have declared and opened a file stream for your output file, you can write data to that file using the **file insertion operator** (<<). Using the insertion operator with a file stream works the same way as using it with `cout`, the standard output stream. Example 2-11 shows a program that writes data to a file.

Example 2-11

```
// Ex2-11.cpp
// This program writes data to a file.

#include <fstream.h>
#include <iostream.h>
int main()
{
  char ch1 = 'U';
  char ch2 = 'R';
  short int age = 29;
  ofstream outAges;
  // Open the file. If the file does not exist it will
```

```
    // be created. If the file exists, it will be
    // overwritten.
    outAges.open("A:\\Chapter2\\ages.dat");

    outAges << ch1 << ' ' << ch2 << ' ' << age << \
      " years old." << endl;
    cout << ch1 << ' ' << ch2 << ' ' << age \
      << " years old." << endl;
    outAges.close();
    return 0;
}
```

The output sent to the screen is U R 29 years old.
The contents of ages.dat is U R 29 years old.

You can use the **put(ch) function** to write a single character to the output stream, where ch is the name of a variable of type char that you declared in your program or a character constant. Example 2-12 shows a program in which the put(ch) function writes data to a file.

Example 2-12

```
// Ex2-12.cpp
// This program writes data to a file
// using the put() function.

#include <fstream.h>
#include <iostream.h>
int main()
{
  char ch1 = 'U';
  char ch2 = 'R';
  short int age = 29;
  ofstream outAges;
  // Open the file. If it does not exist,
  // it will be created.
  // If the file exists, it will be overwritten.
  outAges.open("A:\\Chapter2\\ages2.dat");
  outAges.put(ch1);
  outAges.put(' ');
  outAges.put(ch2);
  outAges.put(' ');
  outAges << age;
  outAges << "years old." << endl;
  cout << ch1 << ' ' << ch2 << ' ' << age << \
    " years old." << endl;
  outAges.close();
  return 0;
}
```

The output sent to the screen is U R 29 years old.
The contents of ages.dat is U R 29 years old.

Exercises

Exercise 2.15 ▶

Write a C++ program exactly like the program described in Exercise 2-14, but change the program to display the output within a box. You can use any character to create a box, such as the * or the _ character. Save the modified program in a file named Ch2-15a.cpp in the Chapter2 folder on your Student Disk.

Exercise 2.16 ▶

The C++ program stored in the file named Ch2-16.cpp is intended to help you with your investments. You have $1,200 to invest each month. You decide to invest your money by buying stock in the Wizard Software Company. Because the price of the stock is highly volatile, you need to calculate how much stock you can purchase each month. Your program should calculate the amount of stock you can buy based on the current price of the stock. You will enter the current stock price each month when you run the program. Your program should provide attractively formatted output that indicates how much stock you can buy this month. Unfortunately, the program is not compiling correctly, so you cannot test its accuracy. Find and fix the errors so that the program runs correctly. Save the corrected program in a file named Ch2-16a.cpp in the Chapter2 folder on your Student Disk.

Exercise 2.17 ▶

Write a C++ program that reads three integer values provided by the user. Find the sum and the average of the three numbers. Display the three integers, their sum, and their average on the screen using the output format of your choice. In addition, write the three integers, their sum, and their average to a file named outNums.dat in the Chapter2 folder on your Student Disk. Save your program in a file named Ch2-17a.cpp in the Chapter2 folder on your Student Disk.

The File Extraction Operator (>>)

After declaring and opening a file stream for your input file, you can read data into your program from the file using the **file extraction operator** (>>). The extraction operator works the same way with a file stream as it does with the `cin`, standard input stream. Example 2-13 shows a program that reads data from an input file.

Example 2-13

```
// Ex2-13.cpp
// This program reads data from an input file.

#include <fstream.h>
#include <iostream.h>
int main()
{
  char ch1;
  char ch2;
  short int age;
  ifstream inAges;

  inAges.open ("A:\\Chapter2\\ages.dat");
  // Two characters and an age are read
  // from the file.

  inAges >> ch1 >> ch2 >> age;

  cout << ch1 << ' ' << ch2 << ' ' << age \
    << " years old." << endl;
```

```
    inAges.close();
    return 0;
}
```

Output:
```
U R 29 years old.
```

Syntax

▶ input_stream.get(ch);

You can use the **get(ch) input function** to read a single character from the input file stream. Example 2-14 shows a program that uses the get(ch) function.

Example 2-14

```
// Ex2-14.cpp
// This program reads data from an input file.

#include <fstream.h>
#include <iostream.h>
int main()
{
  char ch1;
  char ch2;
  short int age;
  ifstream inAges;

  inAges.open ("A:\\Chapter2\\ages.dat");
  inAges.get(ch1);
  inAges.ignore(1,'\n'); // Skips the space character.
  inAges.get(ch2);
  inAges >> age;
  cout << ch1 << ' ' << ch2 << ' ' << age \
    << " years old." << endl;
  inAges.close();
  return 0;
}
```

Output:
```
U R 29 years old.
```

The ignore() and clear() functions work the same way with a file input stream as they do with the cin, standard input stream. For example, fin.ignore(100,'\n'); will read and discard up to 100 characters from the file input stream or read and discard characters up to a newline character, whichever comes first. Using the following clear() function will clear the file input stream: fin.clear();.

Exercises

Exercise 2.18 ▶

Modify the C++ program described in Exercise 2-17 so that the three integer values called for by the program are read from the file stored in the Chapter2 folder on your Student Disk named inNums.dat. Find the sum and average of the three numbers. Display the three integers, their sum, and their average on the screen using an attractive format of your choice. In addition, write the three integers, their sum, and their average to a file named A:\Chapter2\outNums.dat. Save your program in a file named Ch2-18a.cpp in the Chapter2 folder on your Student Disk.

Exercise 2.19 ▶

The C++ program stored in the Ch2-19.cpp file in the Chapter2 folder on your Student Disk is supposed to read a name, Social Security number, and age entered by a user via the keyboard. The program then prints the name, Social Security number, and age to the screen, placing each item on a separate line. The program does not compile, however, so you do not know whether it produces the desired output. Find and fix the errors so that the program runs correctly. Save the corrected program in a file named Ch2-19a.cpp in the Chapter2 folder on your Student Disk.

Exercise 2.20 ▶

You have been hired by the Plays a Lot Video Game Company to help develop its newest video game. In the game, good guys roam through a cave searching for power packs. Power packs have different colors and different values. Your part of the project should calculate the number of power points acquired by a good guy. Write a C++ program that reads the following information from a file named inGame.dat in the Chapter2 folder on your Student Disk: the number of gold power packs owned by a good guy (an integer); the number of silver power packs owned by a good guy (an integer); and the number of bronze power packs owned by a good guy (an integer). A gold power pack is worth 10 power points, a silver power pack is worth 5 power points, and a bronze power pack is worth 1 power point. Your program should total the number of power points accumulated by the good guy and display this number on the screen using an attractive format. It should then write this information to a file named A:\Chapter2\outGame.dat. Save your program in a file named Ch2-20a.cpp in the Chapter2 folder on your Student Disk.

Closing Files in C++

You can use the **close()** function to close files when they are no longer needed. Example 2-15 shows a program that uses the close() function.

Example 2-15

```
// Ex2-15.cpp
// This program reads data from an input file.

#include <fstream.h>
int main()
{
  char ch1;
  char ch2;
  short int age;
  ifstream inAges;

  inAges.open("A:\\Chapter 2\\ages.dat");

  inAges.get(ch1);
  inAges.get(ch2);
  inAges.ignore(1,'\n');
  inAges >> age;
  cout << ch1 << ' ' << ch2 << ' ' << age \
    << " years old." << endl;
  inAges.close();
  return 0;
}
```

Output: U R 29 years old.

S U M M A R Y

- C++ programs end with a .cpp file extension and must include a main() function. C++ functions begin with { and end with }. C++ is a case-sensitive language.

- The preprocessor statement #include <iostream.h> allows your program to perform input and output.

- You must declare a variable before you can use it. To declare a variable, you give it a name and data type. You can initialize a variable with a value when you declare it. You must initialize constant variables.

- You can use integer constants, floating-point constants, character constants, and string constants in C++ statements.

- Inserting comments in your C++ programs improves their readability.

- C++ has many operators. Operators have precedence and associativity.

- Expressions combine variables, constants, and operators. When expressions are evaluated, they result in a value.

- C++ statements specify an action to be taken by your program.

- You can use the insertion operator (<<) with the standard output stream (cout) or a file output stream to output values from your C++ program.

- You can use the put() function to output a single character to the standard output stream (cout) or a file output stream.

- You can use manipulators, such as endl and setw(), with the standard output stream (cout) or a file output stream.

- You can use the extraction operator (>>) with the standard input stream (cin) or a file input stream to input values into your C++ program.

- You can use the get() function to get a single character from the standard input stream (cin) or a file input stream.

- You can use the ignore() function to read and discard characters from the standard input stream (cin) or a file input stream.

- You can use the clear() function to clear an input stream.

P R O G R E S S I V E   P R O J E C T S

1. Books and More

In Chapter 1, you used the specifications for the Books and More inventory control system to help understand the application and to begin working on a design for the entire project. In this chapter, you will use your new knowledge of C++ to begin writing the code to implement the project.

In this assignment, you will write a C++ program that prints the bookstore's name along with a list of options available to the users of the system. These options are as follows: sell a book, get a listing of the complete inventory, get inventory information for a single book title, print a daily report, receive a shipment of books, or quit the inventory control system. Your C++ program should display the bookstore's name and the user options in an attractive format.

Your program also should read the following information for one book from a file named inBooks.dat that is saved in the Chapter2 folder on your Student Disk: book number, a unique integer value that identifies a particular book; price, the price of the book; and number of copies sold, an integer that indicates how many copies were sold in one day.

Your program should calculate the total sales (in dollars) for each book based on the data read from the file. It should then display the results in an attractive format, such as the following:

Book Number	Book Price	Copies Sold	Total Sales
7	$15.95	15	$239.25

Your program should write this information to a file named outBooks.dat in the Chapter2 folder on your Student Disk. Save your program as Ch2-pp1.cpp in the Chapter2 folder on your Student Disk.

2. Baseball Simulation

In Chapter 1, you used the specifications for the baseball simulation program to help understand the application and to begin working on a design for the entire project. In this chapter, you will use your new knowledge of C++ to begin writing the code to implement this program.

In this assignment, you will write a C++ program that prints an attractive display to welcome your user to the baseball simulation game. The program also will simulate the announcer, who introduces the names of the two teams playing today by printing their names in an attractive format on the screen. For now, the names of the two teams are the Chicago White Sox and the Detroit Tigers; this will change in later chapters. The announcer will state the win/loss records for the two teams. These data are stored in the inBall.dat file saved in the Chapter2 folder on your Student Disk. You will have to read these data from the file. The data format is as follows: 23 5 22   6, where 23 is the number of wins for the White Sox, 5 is the number of losses for the White Sox, 22 is the number of wins for the Tigers, and 6 is the number of losses for the Tigers.

Your program should declare and initialize three variables: score1 (runs scored by the White Sox), score2 (runs scored by the Tigers), and the inning number. Initialize score1 and score2 to 0 and inning to 1.

Finally, print the inning number and the score of the game in an attractive format. Save the inning number, score1, and score2 to a file named outBall.dat in the Chapter2 folder on your Student Disk. Save your program as Ch2-pp2.cpp in the Chapter2 folder on your Student Disk.

INDEPENDENT PROJECTS

1. Vacation Photos

You have just picked up photos of your vacation developed from three rolls of film. The photo lab developed 23 pictures from the first roll at a cost of $11.27, 26 pictures from the second roll at a cost of $12.35, and 20 pictures from the third roll at a cost of $10.19. You would like to know the total cost of your pictures as well as the cost per picture. Write a C++ program that calculates these costs and then prints the following output, with each value appearing on a separate line: the total number of pictures developed, the total cost for developing your pictures, and the average cost per picture developed. Save your program as Ch2-ip1.cpp in the Chapter2 folder on your Student Disk.

2. Get to Know Your Compiler

In this project you will become familiar with the error messages generated by your compiler. Work through this project one step at a time. After making the changes in each step, save the program as directed, and then compile and run the program. Write down any error messages that appear on your screen.

Enter the following C++ program, and then save it as Ch2-ip2.cpp in the Chapter2 folder on your Student Disk. This program should compile and run correctly.

```cpp
#include <iostream.h>
int main()
{
  int num1 = 5;
  int num2 = 10;
  int result;
  result = num1 * num2;
  cout << num1 << " + " << num2 << " is "\
    << result << "." << endl;
  return 0;
}
```

For each of the following steps, start with the file named Ch2-ip2.cpp in the Chapter2 folder on your Student Disk, make the changes indicated, and then save the file as directed.

   a. Delete the line #include <iostream.h>, and then save the program as Ch2-ip2a.cpp.
   b. Delete the word int before the word main, and then save the program as Ch2-ip2b.cpp.
   c. Delete the parentheses after the word main, and then save the program as Ch2-ip2c.cpp.
   d. Delete the semicolon after the 5 in the line int num1 = 5;, and then save the program as Ch2-ip2d.cpp.
   e. Delete the line return 0;, and then save the program as Ch2-ip2e.cpp.
   f. Change int to integer in the line int num1 = 5;, and then save the program as Ch2-ip2f.cpp.

g. Change the line

```
cout << num1 << " + " << num2 << " is " << result \
   << "." << endl;
```
to the following:

```
cout << num1 , " + " , num2 , " is " , result, \
   "." , endl;
```
Save the program as Ch2-ip2g.cpp.

h. Remove the closing curly brace, and then save the program as Ch2-ip2h.cpp.

Functions and the Scope of Variables

Introduction ▶ You can write C++ programs as a collection of functions—using functions allows you to write modular programs. That is, you can break down large problems into a collection of small problems and then write a function to solve each of the smaller problems. This programming approach avoids duplication of code and lets you write programs that are easier to read, write, debug, and maintain.

You can arrange the collection of functions that make up a C++ program in any order within a file. In addition, you can store functions in multiple files. You can write a C++ function that will behave as a function or a subroutine. As a C++ programmer, you can either write your own functions or use the functions supplied by the system. Functions and subroutines are blocks of code that have a name and perform a specified task. Functions return a value, while subroutines return nothing. In C++, you will write only functions. If you need to use a named block of code that returns nothing, you can write a **void** function—a function that is intended to return nothing. Writing a **void** function is the same as writing a subroutine. You will learn about writing functions in this chapter.

Syntax

return_type func_name (arg_ type(s));

Function Declaration (Function Prototype)

You must declare all functions in your program before you can use them. A **function declaration** (also known as a **function prototype**) should specify the data type of the value it returns and the data type of each of its arguments. You use the keyword `void` as the return data type if the function should return nothing; the `void` keyword is optional when you want to indicate that a function expects no arguments. Make sure that you always type a semicolon at the end of the function declaration.

The compiler uses the function declaration for type checking. The compiler will verify that the function call (or invocation) and the function definition use the correct number and the correct data types. If the declaration, function definition, and function call do not match, the compiler will generate an error. Example 3-1 shows the function prototype for a function named `print_message()`. This function expects one integer argument and returns no value.

Example 3-1

```
void print_message(int);
```

Exercises

Exercise 3.1 ▶

M O D I F Y

Open the Ch3-1.cpp file in the Chapter3 folder on your Student Disk. Study this program and then add the function declaration for the function named `avg()`. Compile and run the program. Write the program output below, and then save the modified program as Ch3-1a.cpp in the Chapter3 folder on your Student Disk.

_____

Exercise 3.2 ▶

D E B U G

Open the Ch3-2.cpp file in the Chapter3 folder on your Student Disk. Study the function declaration and then compile the program. The function declaration contains several syntax errors. Identify these errors and then make the necessary corrections. Recompile the program until it is error-free, and then run the program. Write the program output below, and then save the corrected program as Ch3-2a.cpp in the Chapter3 folder on your Student Disk.

_____

Exercise 3.3 ▶

D E V E L O P

Write the function declaration for a function named `by_two()`. This function expects one argument (an integer) and returns an integer.

Function declaration: _____

Syntax

▶ func_name (optional_args);

Function Call (Function Invocation)

When the compiler encounters a function name in a C++ program, it calls, or invokes, the function, causing program execution to stop in the current or calling function. Program control is then transferred to the function that is being called, and the computer executes the statements in the called function.

When the function finishes its execution, control returns to the point in the calling function at which the call was made. Figure 3-1 shows a program that illustrates a function call.

```
// Fig3-1.cpp
// This program illustrates a function call.


#include <iostream.h>
// Function declaration
void print_message(int);
int main()
{
   int value = 5;
   // Function call
   print_message(value);
   return 0;
}


// Function definition
void print_message(int number)
{
   cout << "value of number is: "\
   << number << "\n";
   return;

}
```

Execution is halted in `main()`

Control is given to the `print_message()` function

Control returns to the calling function

Figure 3-1: Program that uses a function call

If a function returns a value other than void, then the calling program should use the return value.

Example 3-2 shows the by_two() function, which returns an integer that is assigned to a variable named ans. The print_it() function returns void, so nothing is done with the return value.

Example 3-2

```
int ans, value;
int by_two(int);
void print_it(int);


ans = by_two(value);
print_it(ans);
```

Exercise

Exercise 3.4 ▶ Determine whether each of the following C++ statements is a function declaration or a function call.

a. _____ `float avg(int, int);`

b. _____ `avg(num1, num2);`

Syntax
· · · · · · · · · · · · · · ·

▶ return;
   return expression;

The Return Statement

You use a **return statement** to return program control to the calling function and to return a value from the called function to the calling function. A function can return only one value. Although a function might include more than one return statement, only one return statement will actually be executed.

The data type of the returned value must match the data type specified for the return value in the function declaration and the function definition. The return statement is optional for a void function. Example 3-3 shows how you can use the return statement in a C++ program.

Example 3-3

```
return;
return 'a';
return 1;
return (a + b + c);
```

Exercise

Exercise 3.5 ▶ Add a return statement to the following function.

```
double divide_by_five(int num)
{
  double result;
  result = num / 5.0;
  // Return statement goes here.

}
```

Function Arguments

You use **function arguments** to pass information to a function. The function call must use the correct number and data type for the arguments, and the arguments must appear in the correct order.

Function arguments are considered to be **local** to the function. The term "local" refers to the scope of the argument. Variables and arguments with a local **scope** can be accessed within the block in which they are created. You will learn more about local variables later in this chapter.

Arguments are passed by value. To **pass by value** means that a copy of the argument's value is passed to the function. Arguments that are passed by value serve as input for the function. The called function cannot change the value of the actual argument in the calling function.

Example 3-4 shows a C++ program that contains a function declaration and a function call with arguments that are passed by value.

Example 3-4

```
// Ex3-4.cpp
// Calculates a salary increase.
#include <iostream.h>
double increase(double, double);   //Function declaration
int main()
{
  double salary = 50000.00, raise = 0.15;
  double new_salary;

  cout << "Salary is : " << salary << '.' << endl;
  // A copy of the value of the variables named
  // salary and raise are passed to the increase()
  // function. salary and raise are local to main().
  new_salary = increase(salary, raise);
  cout << "New salary is: " << new_salary << '.' << endl;
  return 0;
}
// Function definition.
// Copies of the values passed to this function
```

```
// are stored in amt and rate.
// amt and rate are local to the increase() function.
double increase(double amt, double rate)
{
  double new_value;
  new_value = amt * (1 + rate);
  return new_value;
}
```

Exercises

Exercise 3.6 ▶

Open the Ch3-6.cpp file in the Chapter3 folder on your Student Disk. Study this program and then add the necessary function declarations and function calls. Compile and run the program. Write the program output below, and then save the modified program as Ch3-6a.cpp in the Chapter3 folder on your Student Disk.

Exercise 3.7 ▶

D E B U G

Open the Ch3-7.cpp file in the Chapter3 folder on your Student Disk. Study the function calls and the function definitions, and then compile the program. The function calls and function definitions contain several syntax errors. Identify these errors and then make the necessary corrections. Recompile the program until it is error-free, and then run it. Write the program output below, and then save the corrected program as Ch3-7a.cpp in the Chapter3 folder on your Student Disk.

Exercise 3.8 ▶

D E V E L O P

Write the function declaration and a valid function call for a function named cube_it(). This function expects one integer argument and returns an integer.

Function declaration: _____

Function invocation: _____

Syntax
· · · · · · · · · · · · · · ·

▶ return_type
    function_name(argument_list)
    {
      declarations;
      statement(s);
    }

Function Definition

A **function definition** is a named block of code. A block of code is defined by opening and closing curly braces ({ and }). You can use arguments to pass data to such a function, which then returns a single value.

A function definition should specify its return data type. It should also specify the data type of each of its arguments and assign a name to each argument. The same rules apply to naming functions that apply to naming variables. That is, function names can contain alphabetic characters, digits, and underscores, but they cannot begin with a digit. Example 3-5 shows the function definition for the print_value() function.

Example 3-5

```
void print_value(int number)
{
  cout << "The value of number is " << \
    number << '.' << endl;
}
```

Exercises

Exercise 3.9 ▶

Open the Ch3-9.cpp file in the Chapter3 folder on your Student Disk. Study this program and then add the function definition for the add_em() function. Write a function to calculate the sum of the three arguments and then return the sum. Print the sum in the main() function. Compile and run the program. Write the program output below, and then save the modified program as Ch3-9a.cpp in the Chapter3 folder on your Student Disk.

Exercise 3.10 ▶

Open the Ch3-10.cpp file in the Chapter3 folder on your Student Disk. Study this program and then compile it. The function definition of the three_times() function contains several syntax errors. Identify these errors, make the necessary corrections, and then recompile the program. (You can assume that the function declaration is correct.) When the program compiles without any errors, run it. Write the program output below, and then save the corrected program in a file named Ch3-10a.cpp in the Chapter3 folder on your Student Disk.

Exercise 3.11 ▶

Write a C++ program with a main() function that gets the following input from a user: department number (short), hourly rate (double), and hours worked (short). Write a function named calc_pay() that is called from main() and multiplies the hourly rate by the hours worked to calculate a weekly salary. The calc_pay() function should return the weekly salary. Print the weekly salary from within the main() function. Also print the department number, hourly rate, and hours worked in the main() function. Save the program as Ch3-11a.cpp in the Chapter3 folder on your Student Disk.

Using Standard Library Functions

A **library** is a collection of shared functions that you can use in many programs. The C++ compiler provides many such functions. To use the library functions, you need to know the function's name, its purpose, the number of arguments it expects and the data types of the arguments, the value returned by the function and its data type, and the header file (.h) that you should #include to ensure that your program will have access to the correct function declaration for the function. (You will learn more about header files in Chapter 9.) The following library functions are supplied with most C++ compilers: input/output, string handling, character handling, dynamic memory allocation, general, and math. The pow() function, for example, is a standard library function that you can use to raise a number to a power of two, three, and so on. Example 3-6 shows the function declaration for this function and a C++ program that uses the pow() function.

Example 3-6

```
double pow(double, double);
```

The function declaration for pow() is found in <math.h>. The function expects two arguments, both of which are doubles. The function returns a double, which is the value of the first argument raised to the power of the second argument.

```
// Ex3-6.cpp
// C++ program that uses the pow() function.
#include <iostream.h>
#include <math.h>
```

```
int main()
{
  double number1 = 5.0;
  double number2 = 3.0;
  double result;

  result = pow(number1, number2);

  cout << number1 << " raised to the power of "\
    << number2 << " is "\
    << result << '.' << endl;
  return 0;
}
```

Exercises

Exercise 3.12 ▶

Open the Ch3-12.cpp file in the Chapter3 folder on your Student Disk. Study this program and then add what is needed to use the `sqrt()` function correctly. Compile and run the program. Write the program output below, and then save the modified program as Ch3-12a.cpp in the Chapter3 folder on your Student Disk.

Exercise 3.13 ▶

Open the Ch3-13.cpp file in the Chapter3 folder on your Student Disk. The programmer is trying to change a lowercase letter to an uppercase letter with the `toupper()` function. Make the corrections needed so that you can use the function correctly. Compile and run the program. Write the program output below, and then save the corrected program as Ch3-13a.cpp in the Chapter3 folder on your Student Disk.

Exercise 3.14 ▶

Write a C++ program that generates a random number between 1 and 10 and then prints the number. Compile and run your program. You will have to research the C++ `rand()` and `srand()` functions to complete this assignment. Save the program as Ch3-14a.cpp in the Chapter3 folder on your Student Disk.

Variable Scope

The **scope** of a variable dictates the section of the program where the variable is known or can be accessed, and therefore used. Variables can have either local or global scope. If a variable has local scope, it can be used only in the block in which it is declared. As noted earlier, in C++, opening and closing curly braces define a block. If a variable has **global scope**, it is declared outside of the curly braces; this type of variable is then known and can be used from the point in the file where it is declared until the end of the file.

Example 3-7 illustrates the declaration and use of global and local variables in a C++ program.

Example 3-7

```
// Ex3-7.cpp
// Illustrates using local and global variables
// in a C++ program.
#include <iostream.h>
```

```cpp
// Global function declaration; now any C++
// statement that follows can invoke this function.
void func(void);
// Global variable, known from this point
// to the end of the file.
int num1;

int main()
{
  int num2;  // Local to main()
  num1 = 5;  // Changes value of global variable
  num2 = 20; // Changes value of local variable

  cout << "Main: Value of num1 is " << num1 \
    << '.' << endl;
  cout << "Main: Value of num2 is " << num2 \
    << '.' << endl;

  func();  // Function call

  cout << "Main: Value of num1 is " << num1 \
    << '.' << endl;
  cout << "Main: Value of num2 is " << num2 \
    << '.' << endl;

  return 0;
}

void func()
{
  // Local to func(), not the same as num2 in main().
  int num2;

  num2 = 15;      // Changes value of local variable.
  cout << "In func: Value of num1 is " << num1 \
    << '.' << endl;
  cout << "In func: Value of num2 is " << num2 \
    << '.' << endl;
  num1 = 30;      // Changes value of global variable.

  return;
}
```

Output:
```
Main: Value of num1 is 5.
Main: Value of num2 is 20.
In func: Value of num1 is 5.
In func: Value of num2 is 15.
Main: Value of num1 is 30.
Main: Value of num2 is 20.
```

Storage Classes

The **storage class** of a variable affects its scope, its lifetime, and its location in memory. The **scope** of a variable determines where a variable is known in a program. The **lifetime** of a variable refers to the length of time that a variable remains available in a program.

C++ includes four storage classes: `automatic`, `register`, `external`, and `static`. Example 3-8 shows different ways to specify a storage class for a variable.

Example 3-8

```
auto int num;
static double miles;
register int distance;
extern float price;
```

The `automatic` Storage Class

The scope of an `automatic` variable includes only the block in which it is declared. The lifetime of an `automatic` variable is the lifetime of the block. An `automatic` variable is created when the block is entered; it is destroyed when the block is exited. The system does not initialize variables of storage class `auto` (which is short for `automatic`). Instead, the programmer must initialize `auto` storage class variables. The `auto` storage class is the default for local variables.

In Example 3-9, the `number1` variable is explicitly declared as an `auto`. The `number2` variable is an `auto` by default, because no storage class was explicitly requested.

Example 3-9

```
auto int number1;
int number2;
```

Exercise

Exercise 3.15 ▶ What is the output of the following C++ program?

```
#include <iostream.h>
int main()
{
  void try_auto();
  short num = 0;

  try_auto();
  num++;
  try_auto();
  num++;
  try_auto();
  num++;
  cout << "In main: value of num is: " << num \
    << '.' << endl;
  return 0;
}
```

```
void try_auto()
{
  int num = 0;

  cout << "try_auto: value of num is: " << num \
    << '.' << endl;
  num++;
  return;
}
```

Output: _____

_____

_____

_____

Syntax
· · · · · · · · · · · · · · ·
▶ register int counter;

The `register` Storage Class

Variables of the `register` storage class have the same scope and lifetime as `auto` variables. The values of `register` storage class variables, however, will be placed in machine registers (hardware) rather than in memory. Registers may be accessed more rapidly than memory, and this strategy can improve the speed and efficiency of programs. The best candidates for registers are variables that are used often, such as loop counters and array indexes.

The number of registers available is small and machine-dependent. The compiler will switch `register` variables to the storage class `auto` automatically if a register is not available or is not supported.

The `external` (Global) Storage Class

An `external` or global variable is declared outside a function. Global variables are available to all functions that follow their declaration in a file. They are initialized to zero when the program is compiled, and they continue to exist until the program stops executing. You should be careful when using global variables, because *all* functions can access and change them—not just the functions that *should* have access.

Similar to global variables, function declarations that appear outside a function are considered global. They can be used by all the functions that follow them in the file.

Exercises

Exercise 3.16 ▶ What is the output of the following C++ program?

```
#include <iostream.h>
// External variable declarations
int a = 1, b = 2, c = 3;
```

```
int func();   // External function declaration

int main()
{
  int value;

  value = func();
  cout << "Value of value is: " << value << '.' << endl;
  cout << "Value of a is: " << a << '.' << endl;
  cout << "Value of b is: " << b << '.' << endl;
  cout << "Value of c is: " << c << '.' << endl;
  return 0;
}

int func()
{
  int b, c;    // Local to func()
  a = 4;
  b = a;
  c = b;
  return (a + b + c);
}
```

Output: _____

_____

_____

_____

Exercise 3.17 ▶

D E V E L O P

Write a C++ program with a main() function and an add_em() function. The add_em() function should accept three variables of type double, find their sum, and store the value of the sum in an external variable. The main() function should print the sum. Save the program as Ch3-17a.cpp in the Chapter3 folder on your Student Disk.

Multiple Source Files You can store a C++ program in more than one file. The compiler will compile multiple C++ source code files to create a single executable file. The method used to compile multiple files is compiler-dependent. Refer to your compiler's documentation or ask your instructor for more information.

Although a global variable has only one definition, it can have many declarations. The definition allocates memory (storage) space but a declaration does not. You use a declaration to inform the compiler that the variable is defined somewhere else in the program but will be used in a function defined in the file. Using the keyword extern in the declaration prevents the program from generating an undefined symbol error message when the variable is used in a file in which it was not defined.

Figure 3-2 shows a C++ program stored in two files and the use of the extern keyword.

```
// file1.cpp                          // file2.cpp

int price; // Definition              void func3();
float yield; // Definition            void func4();
void func1();                         double interest;  //Definition;
void func2();                                           //available in
                                                        //rest of file
int main()                            extern int price; // Declaration;
{                                                       // available in
  func1();                                              // rest of file
  func2();                            void func3()
  func3();                            {
  func4();                              // Statements
  return 0;                           }
}

// Declaration; available
// in rest of file                    void func4()
                                      {
extern double interest;                 //Declaration; available in
                                        // func4 only
void func1()                            extern float yield;
{                                     }
  //Statements
}

void func2()
{
  //Statements
}
```

Figure 3-2: Use of the extern keyword in a program that is stored in two files

Exercise 3.18 ▶   What is the output of the following C++ program?

```
// Contents of file1.cpp
#include <iostream.h>
int val1 = 1, val2 = 2, val3 = 3;
int func1();
int main()
{
  int retval;
  retval = func1();
  cout << "Value of retval is: " << retval << endl;
  return 0;
}

// Contents of file2.cpp
int func1()
{
  extern int val1;
  int val2, val3;
  val3 = 10;
  val2 = val3;
  val1 = val2;
  return (val1 + val2 + val3);
}
```

Output: _____

Exercise 3.19 ▶

In this exercise you will write two programs. Each program requires a `main()` function and an `add_em()` function. The `add_em()` function adds three values to find their sum. Three variables should be initialized in `main()` and passed to `add_em()`, which then adds them to find their sum.

  a. Put the `main()` and `add_em()` functions in different files. The `add_em()` function should return the sum to `main()` as a double. Print the value of the sum in `main()`. Save the two files as Ch3-19a1.cpp and Ch3-19a2.cpp in the Chapter3 folder on your Student Disk.

  b. Put the `main()` and `add_em()` functions in different files. The value of the sum should be stored in a global variable. Print this value in `main()`. Save the two files as Ch3-19b1.cpp and Ch3-19b2.cpp in the Chapter3 folder on your Student Disk.

The `static` Storage Class

The lifetime of a `static` storage class variable is equivalent to the life of the program. Variables of this storage class are initialized to zero values.

The `static auto` variables differ from `static external` variables. When you create a variable as a `static automatic`, the lifetime of the `automatic` variable becomes the lifetime of the program.

When you create a variable as a `static external`, the scope changes, making the variable available from its declaration to the end of the file but unavailable to other files (even using the keyword `extern`). Variables that are `static` retain their values throughout the program.

Exercise

Exercise 3.20 ▶

What is the output of the following C++ program?

```cpp
// static.cpp
// Using static variables
#include <iostream.h>
void try_stat();

int main()
{
  int num = 1;
  try_stat();
  num++;
  try_stat();
  num++;
  try_stat();
  num++;
  cout << "In main: Value of num is: " << \
    num << '.' << endl;
  return 0;
}
```

```
void try_stat()
{
  static int num = 0;
  cout << "In try_stat: Value of num is: " << \
    num << '.' << endl;
  num++;
  return;
}
```

Output: _____

_____

_____

_____

Variables and Memory

Global and `static` variables are stored in an area of memory called the **data area**. An `automatic` variable is stored in an area of memory known as the **stack**. A `register` variable is not stored in memory, but rather in a hardware register.

Pass by Reference

Passing an argument to a function **by reference** allows the called function to access a variable in the calling function. In other words, the called function gains the ability to change the value of a local variable in the calling function. The argument in the called function becomes an **alias** for the variable in the calling function.

The `&` (ampersand) operator is used in the function declaration and function definition to specify that this argument is passed by reference. The function is called in the same manner as functions whose arguments are passed by value. Example 3-10 shows a program that passes arguments to a function by reference.

Example 3-10

```
// Ex3-10.cpp
// Passing arguments by reference
#include <iostream.h>
//Function declaration, uses & for pass by reference
void increase(double, double, double&);
int main()
{
  double salary=50000.00, raise=0.15, new_salary;

  cout << "Salary is: " << salary << '.' << endl;

  // Call the increase function. The values of the
  // variables salary and raise are passed by value and
  // new_salary is passed by reference.
  increase(salary, raise, new_salary);

  cout << "New salary is: " << new_salary << '.' << endl;
  return 0;
}

// The increase function receives copies of the
// values of salary and raise. The values are stored
// in amt and pcnt. new_salary is passed by reference,
// so new_sal is an alias for new_salary.
```

```
void increase(double amt, double pcnt, double& new_sal)
{
  // Changes value of new_salary in main() function
  new_sal = amt * (1 + pcnt);
  return;
}
```

Exercises

Exercise 3.21 ▶

Open the Ch3-21.cpp file in the Chapter3 folder on your Student Disk. Study this program and then write the swap() function. This function expects two arguments passed by reference and swaps the values of these arguments. Compile and run the program. Write the program output below, and then save the modified program as Ch3-21a.cpp in the Chapter3 folder on your Student Disk.

Exercise 3.22 ▶

Open the Ch3-22.cpp file in the Chapter3 folder on your Student Disk. This program should print the area of a rectangle. Although the program compiles, the output is incorrect. Find the errors and correct them. Remember to pass arguments by reference. Compile and run the program. Write the program output below, and then save the corrected program as Ch3-22a.cpp in the Chapter3 folder on your Student Disk.

Exercise 3.23 ▶

In this exercise, you will write four C++ programs. Each program requires that you write a main() function and an add_em() function. The add_em() function adds three values to find their sum. Save the programs as Ch3-23a.cpp, Ch3-23b.cpp, Ch3-23c.cpp, and Ch3-23d.cpp in the Chapter3 folder on your Student Disk.

  a. Write add_em() to accept three integers and print their sum.
  b. Write add_em() to accept three integers, find their sum, and return the sum to main(). Print the sum in main().
  c. Change add_em() so that it accepts three doubles and returns their sum to main() as a double. Print the sum in main().
  d. Rewrite main(). Declare and initialize three integer variables that you will pass by value to add_em(). Declare another integer variable to store the sum. Pass this variable by reference to add_em(), enabling its contents to be changed in add_em(). Print the sum in main().

Overloading Functions

You can **overload** functions by giving the same name to more than one function. The functions must have different numbers of arguments or the arguments must be of a different data type. C++ will figure out which function to call based on its arguments—this is known as the function's **signature**. The signature of an overloaded function consists of the function name and the argument list; it does not include the function's return type. C++ also will try to match a function's signature by using standard type conversions—for example, an integer argument can be converted to a double.

Overloading functions allows a C++ programmer to choose the most meaningful name for a function. It also permits the use of polymorphic code. The word *polymorphic* is derived from the Greek words *poly*, meaning "many," and *morph*, meaning "form." Polymorphic functions in C++ can take many forms. You will learn more about polymorphism when you begin to use C++ to write object-oriented programs.

For now, you can use function overloading to write functions that perform the same task but with different data types. Example 3-11 shows the function definitions of four overloaded functions named `product()`.

Example 3-11

```
int product(int val1, int val2)
{
  return val1 * val2;
}
int product(int val1, int val2, int val3)
{
  return val1 * val2 * val3;
}
double product(double val1, double val2)
{
  return val1 * val2;
}
double product(double val1, double val2, double val3)
{
  return val1 * val2 * val3;
}
```

Exercises

Exercise 3.24 ▶ Which function declaration would the following function calls match?

```
// Function declarations
#1  int product(int, int);
#2  int product(int, int, int);
#3  double product(double, double);
#4  double product(double, double, double);
// Function calls
                double num1 = 1.0, ans1;
                int num2 = 5, ans2;
_____        ans2 = product(2, 5);
_____        ans1 = product(num1, 2.0, 5.0);
_____        ans1 = product(num1, num1);
_____        ans1 = product(2, 5.0);
_____        ans1 = product(2, 4, num1);
_____        ans2 = product(3, 5, 7);
```

Exercise 3.25 ▶ Write a C++ program that calls two functions, both named `divide_by()`, and then prints the values returned. One of the `divide_by()` functions should

accept two integers; the other should accept two doubles. Both functions should divide the first argument by the second and then return the result. Save your program as Ch3-25a.cpp in the Chapter3 folder on your Student Disk.

Default Function Arguments

In C++, you can assign default values to function arguments. When actual arguments are not provided in the call to a function, C++ will use these default values. The default values for the arguments appear in the function declaration. You must follow one rule when creating default values: Not all arguments need default values, but once a default value has been specified for an argument, all of the subsequent arguments must have a default value as well.

Example 3-12 shows a C++ program with default values specified for the over-loaded functions named product().

Example 3-12

```cpp
// Ex3-12.cpp
// Using default function arguments
#include <iostream.h>
double product(double val1 = 1.0, double val2 = 1.0, \
  double val3 = 1.0);
int product(int val1 = 1, int val2 = 1, int val3 = 1);

int main()
{
  int int_ans, num1 = 5, num2 = 10, num3 = 2;
  double dbl_ans, value1 = 5.0, value2 = 10.0, \
    value3 = 2.0;

  int_ans = product(num1, num2, num3);
  cout << "Value of int_ans is " << int_ans \
    << '.' << endl;

  int_ans = product(num1);
  cout << "Value of int_ans is " << int_ans \
    << '.' << endl;

  dbl_ans = product(value1, value2, value3);
  cout << "Value of dbl_ans is " << dbl_ans \
    << '.' << endl;

  dbl_ans = product(value1);
  cout << "Value of dbl_ans is " << dbl_ans \
    << '.' << endl;
  return 0;
}
// This function finds the product of three doubles.
double product(double v1, double v2, double v3)
{
  return(v1 * v2 * v3);
}
// This function finds the products of three integers.
int product(int v1, int v2, int v3)
{
  return(v1 * v2 * v3);
}
```

Output:
```
Value of int_ans is 100.
Value of int_ans is 5.
Value of dbl_ans is 100.
Value of dbl_ans is 5.
```

Exercises

Exercise 3.26 ▶

D E B U G

Open the Ch3-26.cpp file in the Chapter3 folder on your Student Disk. Study this program, which includes two functions, main() and display(). The main() function reads in three integers: begin, end, and interval. The begin variable represents the first integer to be printed, end represents the last integer to be printed, and interval represents the number of integers to print per line. The display() function prints the output based on the values passed to it. The programmer wants the default number of integers per line to be five. Although the program compiles, the default is not working correctly. Find the errors and correct them. Compile and run the program. Write the program output below, and then save the modified program as Ch3-26a.cpp in the Chapter3 folder on your Student Disk.

Exercise 3.27 ▶

D E V E L O P

Write a C++ program that calls two functions, each named divide_by(). Each divide_by() function divides the first argument passed to it by the second argument passed to it. Both functions return the result of the division. One of the divide_by() functions should accept two integers; the other should accept two doubles. Use default arguments so that if the function is called with one argument, the first argument should be divided by 1. Save the program as Ch3-27a.cpp in the Chapter3 folder on your Student Disk.

S U M M A R Y

■ C++ programs are written as a collection of functions. You must declare all functions before you can use them in a C++ program. A function declaration specifies the data type of the value it returns and the data type of each of its arguments.

■ Functions are called when the name of the function is encountered in a C++ program. A function returns a value. In C++, a function that is written not to return a value is called a void function.

■ Arguments are used to pass information to C++ functions. Arguments are passed by value, which means that the function receives a copy of the value, not the original variable.

■ A function definition is a named block of code that performs a task.

■ C++ programmers can write their own functions or use standard library functions that are supplied with the compiler. Standard library function declarations are found in header files.

■ You should #include header files when you want to use standard library functions.

■ The scope of a variable dictates the section of the program where a variable can be accessed. The lifetime of a variable represents the length of time that a variable remains accessible to a program.

- The storage class of a variable affects its scope, its lifetime, and its location in memory. C++ includes four storage classes: `automatic`, `register`, `external`, and `static`.

- You also can pass arguments by reference. Use the ampersand (`&`) after the data type in the function declaration and function definition to specify pass by reference.

- C++ allows a programmer to overload functions. This means you can write more than one function that has the same name.

- C++ allows a programmer to provide default function arguments.

PROGRESSIVE PROJECTS

1. Books and More

In Chapter 2, you began writing the Books and More inventory system. You printed a banner that displayed the name of the program on the screen and a menu of choices available to the user of the program, and you read data about one book from a file and calculated total sales for that book based on the data.

Now that you know how to use functions, you can add more functionality to the Books and More inventory control system and refine the program created in Chapter 2. In this assignment, you will write the following functions:

- `intro()`: This function prints the bookstore's name along with a list of options available to system users. You performed this task in the `main()` function in Chapter 2.
- `read_inv()`: This function reads data from the inventory file and then prints this information to the screen. For now, the inventory will contain information about one book. The input file, inBooks.dat, is saved in the Chapter3 folder on your Student Disk. You will read the following information from inBooks.dat:

  - Book number: A unique integer value that identifies a particular book
  - Price: The price of the book
  - Number of copies sold: An integer representing how many copies of the book are sold in one day

You also will write a function to handle each of the actions that a user can choose, such as print a list of the entire inventory, print a list of one item in the inventory, sell one item, accept a delivery, and print the daily report. For now, these functions should contain a single statement indicating that the function has been called—for example, your program should print a message noting that the daily report function has been called when it is called. This type of function is called a stub and will change as the development of the inventory system proceeds.

Your `main()` function should make calls to the other functions you have written to test them.

Save your project as Ch3-pp1.cpp in the Chapter3 folder on your Student Disk.

2. Baseball Simulation

You began writing the baseball simulation program in Chapter 2. You simulated the announcer by printing a banner that displayed the names of the two teams playing today and by printing the number of wins and losses for both teams. You read the win and loss data from a file. You also created and initialized some variables and saved their values to an output file.

Now that you know about functions, you can refine the program begun in Chapter 2. In this assignment, you will write the following functions:

- `begin()`: This function simulates the announcer, who identifies the names of the two teams playing today. The names of the teams are the Chicago White Sox and the Detroit Tigers. This work was performed by the `main()` function in Chapter 2.
- `pitch()`: This function will simulate the pitcher throwing the ball to the batter. The `pitch()` function will determine whether the pitcher throws a curveball, fastball, sinker, or a slider. For now, it should contain four statements that announce what type of pitch the pitcher threw. For example, one of the statements would be:

```
cout << "That was a curveball." << endl;
```

- `win_loss()`: This function will announce the teams' win/loss records just as you did in Chapter 2, but will now call the `win_loss()` function to perform the actual work.
- `print_results()`: This function prints the inning number and the score of the game.
- `save_data()`: This function saves the inning number, `score1`, and `score2` to the outBall.dat file just as you did in Chapter 2, but now calls the function `save_data()` to do the work.

■ `main()`: This function declares and initializes three variables: `score1`, `score2`, and `inning`. Initialize `score1` and `score2` to zero and `inning` to 1. The `main()` function should then call the functions you created to test them.

Save your project as Ch3-pp2.cpp in the Chapter3 folder on your Student Disk.

INDEPENDENT PROJECTS

1. Operating System—Copy Command

Commands are part of an operating system. An operating system command allows you to perform many tasks, such as listing the files in a folder, viewing the contents of a file, or making a copy of a file.

Simply Software, Inc. recently hired you as a programmer. Simply Software is developing a new microcomputer operating system named SOS (Speedy Operating System). Your first assignment is to write the copy command, which users will use to make a copy of an existing file.

In the initial implementation of the copy command, you decide to open the existing file by specifying the name of a file in the program. You also decide to specify the name of the new file (which is the copy) in your program. You know that you will need to change the hard-coding of the filenames, but you intend to make this change after the program is working correctly using the hard-coded filenames.

Your C++ program will have three functions: `main()`, `copy()`, and `print_em()`. The `main()` function will act as a driver, calling the `copy()` and `print_em()` functions. The `copy()` function will open two files whose names are hard-coded in the open statements. The existing file, inFile.dat, is saved in the Chapter3 folder on your Student Disk. You will read the contents of the existing file and write its contents to the new file named outFile.dat, which should be saved in the Chapter3 folder on your Student Disk. For now, the existing file contains one line: an integer, a double, and three characters. The current contents of the file are as follows: `1234567 12345.67 one`. Next, you will close the files. Your `print_em()` function will open the two files again, print their contents to the screen, and then close the files. You can determine that your copy command is working correctly by comparing the output. The contents of the two files should be the same because you made a copy of an existing file. Save your C++ program as Ch3-ip1.cpp in the Chapter3 folder on your Student Disk.

2. Super Sales Conference

You are a programming intern at the Super Sales national conference in Dallas, Texas. Your manager has asked you to write a C++ program that attendees can use to register for the conference. Your program should display a welcome screen to the user and then prompt the user for his or her employee ID number (an integer), corporate ID number (an integer), and registration type (the letter *A* for active employees and the letter *R* for retired employees). Your program should display the following information in an attractive manner: employee ID number, corporate ID number, and registration type. Write functions to perform each of these tasks in your program. Save your program as Ch3-ip2.cpp in the Chapter3 folder on your Student Disk.

Selection

Introduction ▶ Programmers use selection statements in a C++ program to change the flow of control. Selection statements are also known as branching statements, because they cause the computer to make a decision and then take a branch or a path in the program. The decision is based on whether an expression evaluates to true or false.

In this chapter you will review the `if` statement, the `if else` statement, nested `if` statements, and the `switch` statement. These statements enable you to include paths or branches in your program. You also will review the relational and logical operators, which set up the expressions that allow selection statements to decide which path or branch to take.

Relational Operators

You can use relational operators to construct relational expressions that compare two values. Relational expressions are useful in selection statements because they evaluate to true or false, thereby permitting decision making in your programs. Figure 4-1 shows the relational operators used in C++.

Operator	Meaning
<	Less than
<=	Less than or equal to
>	Greater than
>=	Greater than or equal to
==	Equal to (two equals signs with no space between them)
!=	Not equal to

Figure 4-1: Relational operators in C++

Example 4-1 shows several examples that illustrate the use of relational operators in C++.

Example 4-1

When the value of the variable named `number1` is 10 and the value of the variable named `number2` is 15, then
```
number1 > number2  evaluates to false.
number1 < number2  evaluates to true.
number1 != number2 evaluates to true.
number1 == number2 evaluates to false.
number1 >= number2 evaluates to false.
number1 <= number2 evaluates to true.
```

Exercise

Exercise 4.1 ▶ What is the value of the relational expression based on the value of the grade?

Value of Grade	Relational Expression	Value of Relational Expression
99	grade == 100	_____
98	grade != 100	_____
60	grade < 100	_____
75	grade > 80	_____
75	grade <= 76	_____
75	grade >= 77	_____

Logical Operators

Logical operators enable you to make multiple comparisons in a selection statement. Logical expressions are useful in selection statements because they evaluate to true or false, thereby permitting decision making in your programs. Figure 4-2 lists the logical operators used in C++.

Operator	Name	Description
&&	AND	All expressions must evaluate to true for the entire expression to be true; this operator is written as two & symbols with no space between them.
||	OR	Only one expression must evaluate to true for the entire expression to be true; this operator is written as two I symbols with no space between them.
!	NOT	This operator reverses the value of the expression; if the expression evaluates to false, then reverse it so that the expression evaluates to true.

Figure 4-2: Logical operators in C++

Example 4-2 shows several examples that illustrate the use of logical operators in C++.

Example 4-2

When the value of the variable named `number1` is 10 and the value of the variable named `number2` is 15, then

`(number1 > number2) || (number1 == 10)` evaluates to true.

`(number1 < number2) && (number1 == 10)` evaluates true.

`(number1 != number2) && (number1 == 10)` evaluates to true.

`!(number1 == number2)` evaluates to true.

Exercise

Exercise 4.2 ▶ What is the value of the logical expression based on the value of the grade?

Value of Grade	Logical Expression	Value of Logical Expression
99	`(grade >= 60) &&` `(grade < 70)`	_____
99	`(grade >= 70) ||` `(grade < 80)`	_____
60	`(grade >= 80) &&` `(grade < 90)`	_____
75	`(grade >= 90) ||` `(grade <= 100)`	_____

The `if` Statement

The **if statement** is a single-path decision statement. That is, if the expression in parentheses evaluates to true, then the computer will execute statementA. If the expression in parentheses evaluates to false, then the computer will not execute statementA. A C++ statement can be either a simple statement or a block statement. A block statement comprises multiple C++ statements. C++ defines a block as statements placed within curly braces. Example 4-3 shows several examples that use `if` statements.

Example 4-3

```cpp
if(pitch == 3)
  cout << "That was a curveball." << endl;

number1 = 10;
remainder = number1 % 2;
if(remainder == 0)
  cout << number1 << " is an even number." << endl;

if(value < 10 || value > 20)
{
  cout << "Incorrect value entered." << endl;
  cout << "Values must be between 10 and 20." << endl;
}
```

Exercises

Exercise 4.3 ▶

Tastes Great Candy Company uses a C++ program to determine how many pieces of candy to pack in a two-pound container. The individual candies weigh one, two, or four ounces. Next month, Tastes Great will begin selling one-pound containers as part of its new product line. Your manager has asked you to change the existing program so that it can determine the number of candies to pack in the new one-pound container. Study the program saved as Ch4-3.cpp in the Chapter4 folder on your Student Disk, and then make the changes needed for the one-pound container. (*Hint:* You will have to ask for additional input.) Save the modified program as Ch4-3a.cpp in the Chapter4 folder on your Student Disk.

Exercise 4.4 ▶

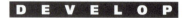

Far Horizons Travel Agency uses a C++ program to calculate the cost of a vacation based on the vacation type and duration (in days). Type A vacations cost $250 per day; Type B vacations cost $150 per day. Each vacation includes the cost per day plus a one-time service charge of $50. The current program does not calculate the vacation costs correctly. Far Horizons has hired you to identify and correct the program errors. Study the program saved as Ch4-4.cpp in the Chapter4 folder on your Student Disk, and then make the necessary changes. Save the corrected program as Ch4-4a.cpp in the Chapter4 folder on your Student Disk.

Exercise 4.5 ▶

DEVELOP

Play Forever Game Company has hired you to write a program for a new video game. You will create the part of the program that calculates the total number of points that a player earns in the Galaxy Game. Players accumulate points by collecting objects. Objects are assigned the following point values: star—10 points; planet—20 points; asteroid—50 points; and comet—100 points. If a player accumulates more than 5,000 total points during a single game, then he or she earns a 500-point bonus.

Eventually your program will be a function in a larger program and will receive the number of stars, planets, asteroids, and comets collected as arguments. For now, you will simulate the larger program by writing a `main()` function that asks the user to enter the number of stars, planets, asteroids, and comets. Your `main()` function should pass these values to another function that calculates the point total. Print the point total in your `main()` function.

Write this program and save it as Ch4-5a.cpp in the Chapter4 folder on your Student Disk.

The `if else` Statement

Syntax

▶ if (expression)
  statementA;
else
  statementB;

The **if else** statement is a dual-path decision statement. That is, if the expression in parentheses evaluates to true, then the computer will execute statementA. If the expression in parentheses evaluates to false, then the computer will execute statementB. Example 4-4 shows several `if else` statements.

Example 4-4

```
if(pitch == 3)
  cout << "That was a curveball." << endl;
else
  cout << "That was not a curveball." << endl;

number1 = 10;
remainder = number1 % 2;
if(remainder == 0)
  cout << number1 << " is an even number." << endl;
else
  cout << number1 << " is an odd number." << endl;

if((grade >= 0) && (grade < 60))
{
  cout << "You earned an F for this exam." << endl;
  cout << "You need to study more." << endl;
}
else
  cout << "You earned a passing grade." << endl;
```

Exercises

Exercise 4.6 ▶

Tix By Phone representatives sell concert tickets to customers who call to place their orders. The telephone representatives use a C++ program to calculate the amount of the sale. The representative asks the customer for the number of adult tickets, the number of children's tickets, and the concert he or she wants to attend. Based on the customer's answers, the telephone representative provides the following input to the program: the number of adult tickets, the price of an adult ticket, the number of children's tickets, and the price of a child's ticket. The program calculates the price of the tickets, adds a 6 percent sales tax to the ticket total, and then adds a 2 percent service charge to the ticket total. The output of this program is a neatly formatted list of the order. Next month, Tix By Phone will begin selling tickets to plays, which will necessitate changes to the current program. The first change is that the telephone representatives will have to enter a *C* for concert tickets or a *P* for play tickets before entering the other information. The second change is that the printed order will show whether the charge applies to concert tickets or play tickets. Study the program saved in the Ch4-6.cpp file in the Chapter4 folder on your Student Disk, and then make the necessary changes. For now, your output should print on the screen. Save the modified program as Ch4-6a.cpp in the Chapter4 folder on your Student Disk.

Exercise 4.7 ▶

Play Forever Game Company has asked you to modify the point collection program for the Galaxy Game that you created in Exercise 4-5. A player still earns a bonus of 500 points after accumulating 5,000 total points. Now, a player earns an additional 100 points if he or she collects a power pill during a single game session. If the player does not collect a power pill during a single game session, then the program should deduct 100 points from his or her total points. Although you made these changes to the program, it does not calculate the total points correctly. Study the program saved as Ch4-7.cpp in the Chapter4 folder on your Student Disk, and then find and correct the errors. Save the corrected program as Ch4-7a.cpp in the Chapter4 folder on your Student Disk.

Exercise 4.8 ▶

Write a C++ program to determine how much money you can save each month toward the purchase of a new TV. Your program should prompt you to enter the following monthly expenses: rent/mortgage, food, gasoline, car payment, insurance, utilities, clothing, miscellaneous, and savings (other than what you allocate for the TV). It also should prompt you to enter your monthly income. You determine that you can save $200 each month for your TV only when you have at least $300 of discretionary income available after paying all of your monthly expenses. Your program should calculate your discretionary income (the amount of income left after paying the bills) and then show the following information: income, discretionary income, total expenses, and a statement such as "Yes, you can save for your TV this month." or "No, you will have to wait and try again next month." Save your program as Ch4-8a.cpp in the Chapter4 folder on your Student Disk.

Syntax
· · · · · · · · · · · · · · · ·

▶ if (expressionA)
   statementA;
  else if (expressionB)
   statementB;
  else
   statementC;

Nested `if` Statements

You can nest an `if` statement to create a multipath decision statement. If expressionA, which is enclosed in parentheses, evaluates to true, then the computer will execute statementA. If expressionA evaluates to false, then the computer will evaluate expressionB. If expressionB evaluates to true, then the computer will execute statementB. If expressionA and expressionB both evaluate to false, then the computer will execute statementC. Example 4-5 shows several nested `if` statements.

Example 4-5

```
if(pitch == 3)
  cout << "That was a curveball." << endl;
else if(pitch == 2)
  cout << "That was a fastball." << endl;
else if(pitch == 1)
  cout << "That was a slider." << endl;
else
  cout << "That was not a legal pitch." << endl;

cout << "Please enter a character." << endl;
cin.get(character1);
if(character1 == '\n' || character1 == '\t' || character1 == ' ')
  white_space++;
else if(character1 >= 'a' && character1 <= 'z')
  lower_case++;
else if(character1 >= 'A' && character1 <= 'Z')
  upper_case++;
else
  other_chars++;
```

Exercises

Exercise 4.9 ▶

Professor Jane Hacker uses a C++ program she developed to determine the final grades for her computer science students. When she runs the program, Jane enters two test scores and five scores for the five programming projects she assigned during the term. Each score is based on a maximum of 100 points for the test or project. The program calculates the total points and then determines the final letter grade for each student. This term Jane offered an extra-credit assignment that students could complete to add 1 percent of their total points to their total points. She has asked you to modify her grade calculation program to accommodate these extra-credit points. Study the program saved as Ch4-9.cpp in the Chapter4 folder on your Student Disk, and then make the necessary changes. Save the modified program as Ch4-9a.cpp in the Chapter4 folder on your Student Disk.

Exercise 4.10 ▶

You own and operate a dog-grooming business named Clip and Curl. You have developed a C++ program to calculate the total charge for services rendered. You charge $20 for a bath, $25 for a trim, and $30 for a shave. The current program does not calculate the charges correctly. Study the program saved as Ch4-10.cpp in the Chapter4 folder on your Student Disk, and then make the necessary changes. Save the corrected program as Ch4-10a.cpp in the Chapter4 folder on your Student Disk.

Exercise 4.11 ▶

D E V E L O P

Sunil Agrawal owns Speedy Software Company. He has asked you to write a C++ program to calculate his employees' end-of-year bonuses. Annual bonuses at the company are based on the employee's performance rating and the employee's annual salary. The rating system is as follows:

Rating	Bonus
1	6 percent of annual salary
2	4 percent of annual salary
3	2 percent of annual salary
4	None

Your program should prompt Sunil to enter an employee's salary and his or her performance rating. The program should then print the following output: salary, performance rating, and bonus. Create this program, and then save it as Ch4-11a.cpp in the Chapter4 folder on your Student Disk.

Syntax
· · · · · · · · · · · · · · · ·

▶ switch (expression)
{
   case constant: statement(s);
   case constant: statement(s);
   case constant: statement(s);
   default: statement(s);
}

The switch Statement

The switch statement, like the nested if statement, is a multipath selection statement. You use the switch statement to compare an expression with an integer constant. Any expression that evaluates to an integer constant can be used—for example, 10 (an integer constant), 'A' (a character constant), or 150/25 (an integer constant).

    Cases are defined within the switch statement by using the label case and including an integer constant after this label. The computer will evaluate the expression in the switch statement and then compare it with the integer constants following the case labels. If the expression and the integer constant match, then the computer will execute the following statements until it encounters a break statement or a closing curly brace. The break statement causes an exit from the switch statement. You can use the keyword default to establish a case for values that do not match any of the case labels.

    A switch statement offers the advantage of being more readable than nested if statements. The switch statement is also easier to maintain. Example 4-6 illustrates the use of a switch statement in C++.

Example 4-6

```
cout << "Enter F to find an item in inventory." << endl;
cout << "Enter S to sell an item in inventory." << endl;
cout << "Enter L to list all items in inventory." << endl;
cin >> selection;
switch(selection)
{
  case 'F':    find_item();
               break;
  case 'S':    sell_item();
               break;
  case 'L':    list_items();
               break;
  default:     cout << "You entered an invalid option." << endl;
               cout << "Try again." << endl;
}
```

Exercises

Exercise 4.12 ▶

You need to modify the program that you wrote for Clip and Curl in Exercise 4-10 to use a `switch` statement. This program calculates the total charge for services rendered ($20 for a bath, $25 for a trim, and $30 for a shave). Reread the program specification for Exercise 4-10, and then study the program saved as Ch4-12.cpp in the Chapter4 folder on your Student Disk. Make the necessary changes and save the modified program as Ch4-12a.cpp in the Chapter4 folder on your Student Disk.

Exercise 4.13 ▶

Sarah Friedman wrote a C++ program that simulates throwing a pair of dice. The program throws two dice, totals the values shown on the dice, and then reports the total to the user. Sarah's current program does not run correctly, however, and she wants you to help her debug it. Study the program saved as Ch4-13.cpp in the Chapter4 folder on your Student Disk, and then make the necessary changes. Save the corrected program as Ch4-13a.cpp in the Chapter4 folder on your Student Disk.

Exercise 4.14 ▶

Write a C++ program that simulates a calculator. Your program should prompt the user to enter two numbers that are data type double and an operator (+, −, *, or /). Based on the input, your program should add, subtract, multiply, or divide the two input numbers. Write separate functions to perform the addition, subtraction, multiplication, and division operations. Use a `switch` statement in your `main()` function to decide which function to call. Save the program as Ch4-14a.cpp in the Chapter4 folder on your Student Disk.

S U M M A R Y

- ▪ Selection statements are used to change the flow of control in a C++ program.

- ▪ Relational operators are used to write relational expressions in C++ statements.

- ▪ Logical operators are used to make multiple comparisons in selection statements.

- ▪ The `if` statement is a single-path selection statement.

- ▪ The `if else` statement is a dual-path selection statement.

- ▪ Nesting `if` statements allows you to create multipath selection statements.

- ▪ The `switch` statement is another multipath selection statement.

PROGRESSIVE PROJECTS

1. Books and More

In this chapter, you will continue to add to the Books and More inventory control system. In Chapter 3, you added an `intro()` function and a `read_inv()` function that read in a book number, price, and a number indicating how many copies of the book are currently held in the inventory. You also wrote functions for each of the actions that a user of the program can choose, such as printing a list of the entire inventory, selling an item, and so on.

Now you will add to the function to sell a book. You will pass the book number and inventory quantity to the `sell()` function. The `sell()` function should prompt the user to enter the number of copies being sold and then check to see whether enough copies are present in the inventory to accommodate the sale. If enough copies are found, then the function should print the number of copies sold and update the number of copies in the inventory for this book. If too few copies are present, it should print the book number, the number of copies requested for sale, and the number of copies currently in the inventory, along with a message that alerts the user that this transaction cannot be completed. For now, this function must be called from the `read_inv()` function because this is where you have access to the quantity-on-hand data. This will change in future assignments.

Next, you will add to the function that prints the data for one item in the inventory. For now, you will pass the book number, price, and inventory quantity to the `list_one()` function. The `list_one()` function should print the values of book number, price, and quantity formatted in an attractive manner. For now, you must call this function from the `read_inv()` function because this is where you have access to the book number, price, and quantity-on-hand data. This will change in future chapters.

Save the project as Ch4-pp1.cpp in the Chapter4 folder on your Student Disk.

2. Baseball Simulation

In Chapter 3, you wrote functions that simulated the announcer introducing the two teams and announcing their win/loss records, saved the game data, and announced the type of pitch thrown. You also wrote a `main()` function that called these functions.

In this chapter, you will rewrite the `pitch()` function to use the system library functions to generate a random number from 1 to 4. If the random number is 1, then your program will print a message that the pitcher threw a curveball. If the random number is 2, then it will print a message that the pitcher threw a fastball. The number 3 will represent a sinker, and the number 4 will represent a slider.

Next, write a function named `batter_up()` that uses the random number generator to generate a random number between 1 and 4. The number 1 indicates that the batter made contact with the ball and it stayed in fair territory, and the numbers 2 through 4 indicate that the batter did not make contact with the ball or the ball was hit into foul territory. If the batter hits the ball, the random number generator should generate a number between 1 and 16 to indicate the type of hit. The values represent the following hits: 1 or 2 for a single, 3 for a double, 4 for a triple, 5 for a home run, 6 for a bunt, 7, 8, and 9 for a pop out, 10, 11, and 12 for a fly out, and 13, 14, 15, and 16 for a ground out. In the case of a bunt, the random number generator should be used again to generate a number between 1 and 4. The values represent the following: 1 for a bunt single and 2, 3, and 4 for a bunt out.

If the batter does not hit the ball or hits it into foul territory, the random number generator should generate a number from 1 to 5. The values represent the following: 1 or 2 for a ball, 3 for a called strike, 4 for a swing and miss, and 5 for a foul ball.

The `batter_up()` function should print a message indicating how the batter did.

Save your project as Ch4-pp2.cpp in the Chapter4 folder on your Student Disk.

INDEPENDENT PROJECTS

1. Date Translator

Write a C++ program that reads in three integer values that represent a month, date, and a four-digit year. Your program should print the date in one of the following formats depending on the user's input. If the user enters 1, then print the month as a word ("January"), the date as an integer (11), and the year (1999). If the user enters 2, then print the month as a three-letter abbreviation ("Jan."), the date as an integer (11), and the year (1999). If the user enters 3, then print the month as an integer (01), the date as an integer (11), and the year (1999). For example:

Please enter a date (three integers: month, day, year): 12 1 99

How would you like to print your date?
    Month date, full year (January 11, 1999): Enter 1.
    Abbreviated month date, full year (Jan. 1, 1999): Enter 2.
    Month/date/year (12/1/99): Enter 3.

If the user enters 1, then the output would be December 1, 1999.

Create the program, and then save it as Ch4-ip1.cpp in the Chapter4 folder on your Student Disk.

2. File Statistics

Some computer operating systems include a utility that counts the number of lines, words, and characters in a file. You will write a program to count these items in a later chapter. For now, you will write a program that does only counting of characters. Your program should prompt the user to enter seven characters. It should then print the number of alphabetic, numeric, whitespace, and other characters that were entered. For example:

Please enter seven characters: uu33 $$
You entered 2 alphabetic characters
    2 numeric characters
    1 whitespace character
    2 other characters
Please enter seven characters: rr7 % 8
You entered 2 alphabetic characters
    2 numeric characters
    2 whitespace characters
    1 other character

Save the program as Ch4-ip2.cpp in the Chapter4 folder on your Student Disk.

Repetition

Introduction ▶ You use **repetition statements**, or **loops**, in C++ programming to change the flow of control. Repetition statements allow a programmer to direct the computer to execute a statement or group of statements multiple times.

In this chapter, you will review the three types of C++ programming repetition statements: the `while` loop, the `for` loop, and the `do while` loop. You also will review other I/O statements that are used to control loops and other C++ operators that are used in repetition statements.

Increment (++) and Decrement (--) Operators

The C++ increment and decrement operators provide a concise and efficient method for adding 1 or subtracting 1 from an **lvalue**. An **lvalue** refers to an area of memory to which you can write data. You must place an **lvalue** on the left side of an assignment statement, because an assignment statement is actually storing a value at a memory location. For example, the assignment statement x = 10; assigns the value 10 to the variable named x. The value of 10 is then stored at the memory location associated with the variable named x. The increment and decrement operators add 1 or subtract 1 from an **lvalue**, so the statement x++; is equivalent to x = x + 1; and the statement x- -; is equivalent to x = x - 1;. Each of the expressions in these statements changes or writes to the memory location associated with the variable named x.

Both the increment and decrement operators have prefix and postfix forms. When you use the **prefix form**, the **lvalue** is incremented or decremented immediately. When you use the **postfix form**, the **lvalue** is incremented or decremented after it is used. Example 5-1 illustrates the use of the increment operator in C++.

Example 5-1

```
x = 5;
y = x++;   // y is assigned the value of x,
           // then x is incremented.
// Value of x is 6.
// Value of y is 5.

x = 5;
y = ++x;   // x is incremented first,
           // then the value of x is assigned to y.
// Value of x is 6.
// Value of y is 6.
```

Exercise

Exercise 5.1 ▶ What is the output of the following C++ program?

```
#include <iostream.h>
int main()
{
  int x = 10;
  int y;

  cout << "Value of x is " << x++ << '.' << endl;
  cout << "Value of x is " << ++x << '.' << endl;
  y = x++;
  cout << "Value of x is " << x << '.' << endl;
  cout << "Value of y is " << y << '.' << endl;
  x = y- -;
  cout << "Value of x is " << x << '.' << endl;
  cout << "Value of y is " << y << '.' << endl;
  return 0;
}
```

Output: _____

_____

_____

_____

_____

_____

Syntax

• • • • • • • • • • • • • •

▶ while(expression)
   statementA;

The while Loop

The while loop allows you to direct the computer to execute the statement in the body of the loop as long as the expression within the parentheses evaluates to true. The body of the loop can include either a simple statement or a block statement. After the body of the loop executes, the computer evaluates the expression again. If the expression evaluates to true, then the computer executes the body of the loop again. As soon as the expression evaluates to false, the computer will no longer execute the statement in the body of the loop and will continue executing the program with the statement following the loop.

You can use a counter or an event to control a while loop. With a counter, you set up the loop to execute a specified number of times. With an event, the loop is executed until something occurs within the body of the loop that causes the expression to evaluate to false. An event-controlled loop is effective when you do not know how many times the loop will need to execute; it allows the loop to continue to execute until an event occurs. A while loop may execute zero times if the expression evaluates to false immediately. In that case, the computer will not execute the body of the loop at all.

Example 5-2 shows the use of a counter-controlled while loop.

Example 5-2

```cpp
// Ex5-2.cpp
#include <iostream.h>
int main()
{
  const int MAXSTU = 25;
  int num_stu = 0;
  char grade;
  // Get 25 grades and print them.
  while(num_stu < MAXSTU)
  {
    cout << "Enter a grade: ";
    cin >> grade;
    cout << grade << endl;
    num_stu++;
  }
  return 0;
}
```

Example 5-3 shows the use of an event-controlled `while` loop.

Example 5-3

```
// Ex5-3.cpp
#include <iostream.h>
int main()
{
  int digit_chars = 0;
  int other_chars = 0;
  char input;


  cin.get(input);
  while(input != '\n')
  {
    if((input >= '0') && (input <= '9'))
      digit_chars++;
    else
      other_chars++;
    cin.get(input);
  }
  cout << "Number of digit_chars is " << digit_chars  <<
    '.' << endl;
  cout << "Number of other_chars is " <<
  other_chars << '.' << endl;
  return 0;
}
```

Additional I/O Methods

You can use the `eof()` function with `cin` or with an open file. The `eof()` function returns true if EOF (end of file) is read; it returns false if EOF has not been read. This function often is used in a `while` loop to allow the program to read from a file or the keyboard until it encounters EOF. You enter the EOF character by typing Ctrl + Z (for Windows users) or Ctrl + D (for UNIX users). Example 5-4 illustrates the use of the `eof()` function to control a loop. Notice that the `!` operator is needed because `eof()` returns true only when EOF is encountered.

Example 5-4

```
// Ex5-4.cpp
#include <iostream.h>
int main()
{
  char input;
  cout << "Enter a character: ";
  cin >> input;
  while(!(cin.eof()))
  {
    cout << input << endl;
    cout << "Enter another character: ";
    cin >> input;
  }
  return 0;
}
```

You can test cin or an opened file. If the input to cin or infile is valid, then testing cin or infile evaluates to true. If the input is invalid or if EOF was encountered, cin or infile will evaluate to false. You can simplify the program shown in Example 5-4 by changing the condition in the while loop from !(cin.eof()) to (cin), as shown in Example 5-5.

Example 5-5

```
// Ex5-5.cpp
#include <iostream.h>
int main()
{
  char input;
  cout << "Enter a character: ";
  while(cin >> input)
  {
    cout << input << endl;
    cout << "Enter another character: ";
    cin >> input;
  }
  return 0;
}
```

Exercises

Exercise 5.2 ▶

M O D I F Y

Professor Jane Hacker uses a C++ program to calculate a student's letter grade based on the student's two test scores and five program scores. She has asked you to modify her grade program so that she can enter the scores for all students in her Introduction to C++ class. The new program must count the number of A, B, C, D, and F letter grades earned by her students. Professor Hacker has 26 students in her C++ class this term. You should use a while loop in the solution to this problem. The current program is saved as Ch5-2.cpp in the Chapter5 folder on your Student Disk. Study this program and then make the necessary modifications. Save the modified program as Ch5-2a.cpp in the Chapter5 folder on your Student Disk.

Exercise 5.3 ▶

D E B U G

John Huang, the owner of the Really Rhythm Music Store, uses a C++ program to calculate and output the amount of sales tax he should charge a customer based on a subtotal that he enters. The program worked fine until last month, when John modified the program to allow him to enter more than one purchase without restarting the program. Now the program does not execute correctly. John has asked you to find and correct the errors in the program, which is saved as Ch5-3.cpp in the Chapter5 folder on your Student Disk. Save the corrected program as Ch5-3a.cpp in the Chapter5 folder on your Student Disk.

Exercise 5.4 ▶

D E V E L O P

Write a C++ program that gets its input from the file saved as words.dat in the Chapter5 folder on your Student Disk. Your C++ program should read the entire contents of the file and count the number of characters and the number of lines it contains. Report the name of the file, and the number of characters and lines in the file. Remember that you should count newline characters ('\n') as characters. Save your C++ program as Ch5-4a.cpp in the Chapter5 folder on your Student Disk.

Syntax

▶ **do**
   statementA;
  while(expression);

The do while Statement

The do while loop is similar to the while loop, except that the expression is evaluated after the body of the loop executes. As a result, the body of a do while loop always executes at least once. The body of the do while loop will continue to execute as long as the expression evaluates to true. Example 5-6 shows a do while loop in a C++ program.

Example 5-6

```cpp
// Ex5-6.cpp
#include <iostream.h>
int main()
{
  char input;
  do
  {
    cout << "Main Menu" << endl;
    cout << "Enter A to do addition." << endl;
    cout << "Enter S to do subtraction." << endl;
    cout << "Enter M to do multiplication." << endl;
    cout << "Enter D to do division." << endl;
    cout << "Enter Q to quit." << endl;
    cin >> input;
    cout << "Value of input is " << input << '.' << endl;
  }
  while(input != 'Q');
  return 0;
}
```

Exercises

Exercise 5.5 ▶

MODIFY

Rewrite the program described in Exercise 5-2 using a do while loop in your solution, rather than a while loop. Save the modified program as Ch5-5a.cpp in the Chapter5 folder on your Student Disk.

Exercise 5.6 ▶

DEBUG

Your friend, Frank Brown, is taking an Introduction to Programming class. He is working on a programming assignment for which he is getting incorrect output. The program should allow the user to enter two integer values. It is supposed to add the two values and output the two numbers and their sum as many times as required by the user. The user enters EOF (Ctrl + Z for Windows or Ctrl + D for UNIX) to stop the program. Frank has asked you to review his program, which is saved as Ch5-6.cpp in the Chapter5 folder on your Student Disk. What advice would you give Frank about the errors? Do not fix his program.

Exercise 5.7 ▶

DEVELOP

The All-American Cable Company provides your community with cable TV connectivity. The company changes the channel number assignments frequently. Write a program that lets the user look up channel numbers to find the station assigned, or quit the program. You should be able to look up several channel numbers without restarting the program. Last month, the channel assignments were as follows:

Channel Number	Station Name
2	WBBM
5	WMAQ
7	WLS
9	WGN
11	WTTW
40	AE
41	AMC
36	CNN
99	DIS
33	ESPN
15	HBO
26	MAX
18	QVC
27	SHO
49	TNT

Write the program to look up the stations and save it as Ch5-7a.cpp in the Chapter5 folder on your Student Disk.

The for Loop

Syntax

▶ for(exp1; exp2; exp3)
    statementA;

The for loop is a compact method for initializing variables, executing the body of a loop, and changing the contents of variables. It consists of three expressions that are separated by semicolons and enclosed within parentheses. The first time that the computer executes the for loop, the first expression is executed once. Usually, this expression initializes a variable. The computer then evaluates the second expression. If the second expression evaluates to true, the computer executes the body of the loop. If the second expression evaluates to false, then the computer does not execute the body of the loop. After the body of the loop executes, the computer evaluates the third expression. This expression usually increments or decrements the variable that you initialized in the first expression. After the computer evaluates the third expression, then the second expression is evaluated again. If the second expression still evaluates to true, the body of the loop is executed again, and the computer then evaluates the third expression again. This process continues until the second expression evaluates to false.

Example 5-7 shows a for loop in a C++ program.

Example 5-7

```
// Ex5-7.cpp
#include <iostream.h>
int main()
{
  int k;

  for(k = 0; k < 100; k++)
```

```
    {
      if(k % 2 == 0)
        cout << k << " is an even number." << endl;
      else
        cout << k << " is not an even number." << endl;
    }
    return 0;
}
```

You can write `for` loops that do not include any or all of the three expressions, but you always must include the semicolons. If you omit the second expression, however, then it automatically evaluates to true—and you have programmed an infinite loop. Example 5-8 shows several illustrations of `for` loops with omitted expressions.

Example 5-8

```
int max = 10;
int total = 0;

for(k = 0; k < max;)
    // k is incremented in the next statement
    // rather than in expression3.
    total += k++;

cout << "The value of total is " << total << endl;
    // The next statement is an infinite loop
    // because expression2 is omitted.
for(;;)
    run_it();
```

Exercises

Exercise 5.8 ▶

MODIFY

Rewrite the program described in Exercises 5-2 and 5-5 using a `for` loop, rather than a `while` loop or a `do while` loop. Save the modified program as Ch5-8a.cpp in the Chapter5 folder on your Student Disk.

Exercise 5.9 ▶

DEBUG

You have written a C++ program to find the total of the numbers from 0 to 500 that are divisible by 9 or 19. The current program, which is saved as Ch5-9.cpp in the Chapter5 folder on your Student Disk, does not compile, however. Find and correct the errors, and then test the program to verify that it generates the correct output. If the program compiles but does not generate the correct output, find and correct the logic errors. Save your corrected program as Ch5-9a.cpp in the Chapter5 folder.

Exercise 5.10 ▶

DEVELOP

Write a C++ program that finds a weekly average temperature by calculating the average of seven temperatures input by the user. The program should write its output to a file named temps.out using a format that produces a table similar to the one on page 75. Save the program as Ch5-10a.cpp in the Chapter5 folder on your Student Disk.

Day	Temperature
1	22
2	35
3	37
4	31
5	28
6	40
7	42

The Comma Operator

The **comma operator**, which is commonly used in `for` loops, allows you to execute multiple statements as part of a single expression. The C++ code in Example 5-9 uses the comma operator in a `for` loop.

Example 5-9

```
// Ex5-9.cpp
#include <iostream.h>
int main()
{
  int sum = 0;
  const int MAX = 5;
  int j, k;

  for(j = 0, k = 10; j < MAX; j++, k--)
    sum += j + k;
  cout << "Value of sum is: " << sum << '.' << endl;
  return 0;
}
```

Output: `Value of sum is: 50.`

In Example 5-9, the first and third expressions in the `for` loop now include two tasks. In the first expression, the variable named `j` is initialized to 0 and the variable named `k` is initialized to 10. In the third expression, the variable named `j` is incremented and the variable named `k` is decremented. The comma operator accomplishes two tasks in one expression.

Nested Loops

You can nest any C++ loop statements in the body of another loop. Nested loops, for example, are useful when you need to access the values stored in a multidimensional array. You will learn more about arrays and nested loops in Chapter 6. Example 5-10 shows a nested loop in a C++ program.

Example 5-10

```cpp
// Ex5-10.cpp
#include <iostream.h>
int main()
{
  int sum = 0, max_rows = 5, max_cols = 4;
  int rows, columns;

  for(rows = 0; rows < max_rows; rows++)
    for(columns = 0; columns < max_cols; columns++)
      sum += rows + columns;

  cout << "Value of sum is " << sum << << '.' << endl;
  return 0;
}
```

Output: `Value of sum is 70.`

In Example 5-10, the outer `for` loop executes five times. The inner loop executes 20 times—four times in each of the outer loop's five repetitions.

Exercises

Exercise 5.11 ▶

Customers at the Good Life Gym use a C++ program to calculate the number of calories burned in a weight-training workout. When customers finish their workouts, they enter the number of minutes they worked out; the program then calculates the number of calories burned. The program calculates the number of calories burned based on the duration of the workout: two calories burned for the first minute of the workout; three calories per minute during minutes 2 through 10; four calories per minute during minutes 11 through 20; and five calories per minute during minutes 21 through 30.

Joe Lifter, the owner of the Good Life Gym, wants you to modify the program so that it calculates the calories burned for a workout lasting as long as 60 minutes. The new formula is six calories burned per minute during minutes 31 through 40; seven calories per minute during minutes 41 through 50; and eight calories per minute during minutes 51 through 60. The revised program should calculate calories for any number of workouts—the current program requires the customer to restart the program to calculate calories for more than one workout. The current program is saved as Ch5-11.cpp in the Chapter5 folder on your Student Disk. Make the necessary changes, and then save the modified program as Ch5-11a.cpp in the Chapter5 folder on your Student Disk.

Exercise 5.12 ▶

The program saved as Ch5-12.cpp in the Chapter5 folder on your Student Disk is supposed to print the outline of a rectangle that looks like Figure 5-1. Although the program compiles correctly, it does not produce the correct output. Find and fix the logic errors so the program produces the correct output. Save the corrected program as Ch5-12a.cpp in the Chapter5 folder.

Figure 5-1

Exercise 5.13 ▶

D E V E L O P

Ling Chou owns a small computer consulting company that employs five employees who currently work on stand-alone PCs. Ling designed a floor plan for the local area network that he would like to install. He has asked you to write a C++ program to calculate the best place to locate the network server. This location would be the site that requires the least amount of cabling to connect the PCs directly to the server. Each asterisk in Ling's floor plan represents the location of a PC. Write a C++ program that calculates the x and y coordinates of the best location for the server. You can use the distance formula to determine the distance between two points. When coded in C++, the distance formula is `sqrt(pow((x1-x2),2) + pow((y1-y2),2));`. You will have to `#include <math.h>` to use the `sqrt()` and `pow()` functions. Save the program as Ch5-13a.cpp in the Chapter5 folder on your Student Disk. The coordinates of the points where the PCs in the office are located are as follows:

x Coordinate	y Coordinate
15	60
25	90
60	75
75	60
80	25

Figure 5-2 shows Ling's floor plan.

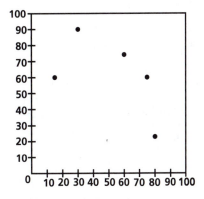

Figure 5-2: Ling's floor plan

Using break and continue Statements

You use a `break` statement in a C++ program to exit from a `while` loop, a `do while` loop, or a `for` loop. In Chapter 4, you learned that the `break` statement also is used in a `switch` statement. When you use a `break` statement to exit a loop, the `break` statement causes an exit from only the innermost loop; it will not exit multiple loops.

You can use a `continue` statement in a `while` loop, a `do while` loop, or a `for` loop. The **continue** statement stops the current iteration of the loop body and starts the next iteration. Figure 5-3 illustrates program flow when using `continue` and `break` statements in a `while` loop, a `do while` loop, and a `for` loop.

```
// Program flow with continue and break.

#include <iostream.h>

int main()
{
  const int MAX = 10;
  int k;
  int total = 0;

  for(k = 0; k < MAX; k++)
  {
    if(k == 6)
             break;
    if(k == 2 || k == 3)
          continue;
    total += k;
  }
  cout << "Value of total is " << total << '.' << endl;

  total = 0;
  k = 0;

  while(k < MAX)
  {
    if(k == 6)
             break;
    if(k == 2 || k == 3)
    {
      k++;
      continue;
    }
    total += k;
    k++;
  }
  cout << "Value of total is " << total << '.' << endl;

  total = 0;
  k = 0;

  do
  {
    if(k == 6)
             break;
    if(k == 2 || k == 3)
    {
      k++;
      continue;
    }
    total += k;
    k++;
  }while(k < MAX);
  cout << "Value of total is " << total << '.' << endl;

  return 0;
}
```

Figure 5-3: Program flow with `continue` and `break` statements

Example 5-11 shows a continue statement and a break statement in a while loop.

Example 5-11

```
// Ex5-11.cpp
#include <iostream.h>
int main()
{
  int lower = 0, num_chars = 0, non_alpha = 0;
  char ch;
  cout <<  "Enter text." << endl;
  while(cin.get(ch))
  {
    num_chars++;
    if(ch <= 'Z' && ch >= 'A')
      continue;   // Current iteration stops.
    else if(ch <= 'z' && ch >= 'a')
      lower++;
    else
    {
      non_alpha++;
      break;  // Exit the loop.
    }
  }
  cout << "Of the " << num_chars << \
    " characters provided as input, " << lower << \
    " were lowercase letters." << endl;
  cout << endl << non_alpha << \
    " was a non-alpha character." << endl;
  cout << endl << num_chars - (lower + non_alpha) << \
    " were uppercase." << endl;

  return 0;
}
```

If the input to this program was ABcdefgHIJklmnOpQrstuvWXYZ!, then the output would be:

```
Of the 27 characters provided as input, 15 were lowercase
letters.
1 was a non-alpha character.
11 were uppercase.
```

Exercises

Exercise 5.14 ▶

You have written a program to figure out which home repairs you will complete this spring using a $20,000 home improvement loan. Your current program uses a break statement. Rewrite the program saved as Ch5-14.cpp in the Chapter5 folder on your Student Disk to eliminate the break statement. Use the following data when running the program. As it is listed in priority order, this information should be entered in the order specified on page 80.

Repair	Amount Required
Roof repair	$3,000
Driveway repair	$2,500
Siding	$8,000
Gutters	$1,500
Rewire basement	$7,000
General painting	$1,000
Landscaping	$1,000
Patio repair	$2,000
Build deck	$3,000

Save this program as Ch5-14a.cpp in the Chapter5 folder on your Student Disk.

Exercise 5.15 ▶

D E B U G

The program saved as Ch5-15.cpp in the Chapter5 folder on your Student Disk is a password verification program that ensures that a user enters a password of at least six characters, including at least two alphabetic characters and one numeric character. As currently written, the program does not recognize valid passwords. Study the program and then correct the errors. Save the corrected program as Ch5-15a.cpp in the Chapter5 folder.

Exercise 5.16 ▶

D E V E L O P

Write a C++ program that reads the contents of the file named in5.dat that is saved in the Chapter5 folder on your Student Disk. Your program should create a new file named out5.dat according the following rules. Save the finished C++ program as Ch5-16a.cpp in the Chapter5 folder.

- If you read a lowercase letter, then write it to the new file.
- If you read an uppercase letter, convert it to lowercase and then write the lowercase letter to the file.
- If you read a newline character, then write two newline characters to the file.
- If you read a space character, then write the space character to the file.
- If you read a tab character, then write a space character to the file.
- Keep a count of all other characters that you read, but do not write them to the file.
- Report the number of characters you did not write to the new file.

S U M M A R Y

- You use repetition statements, or loops, to execute a statement or group of statements multiple times.

- The increment (++) operator and the decrement (– –) operators add 1 to an lvalue and subtract 1 from an lvalue, respectively.

- A while loop executes a statement or group of statements as long as a condition remains true.

- The statement(s) in a while loop might never execute if the condition evaluates to false immediately.

- The eof() function returns true if end of file (EOF) is read; otherwise, it returns false.

- You can test a file input stream or `cin`. They will evaluate to true if no errors have occurred or if EOF has not been read.

- A `do while` loop executes a statement or statements at least once, because the condition that controls the loop is evaluated at the bottom of the loop.

- A `for` loop is usually written to execute a specified number of times.

- The comma operator allows you to execute multiple statements as part of a single expression.

- You can nest any of the three C++ loops within another loop.

- A `break` statement causes an immediate exit from a loop or a `switch` statement.

- A `continue` statement stops the current iteration of a loop and starts the next iteration.

P R O G R E S S I V E   P R O J E C T S

1. Books and More

In this assignment, you will continue to add to the Books and More inventory control system. In Chapter 4, you added a `sell()` function that updated the number of copies in the inventory for one book. It was called from the `read_inv()` function, because the `read_inv()` function is the only place in the program where the information is available. You will change this location in future chapters. You also wrote a `list_one()` function that printed all of the information about one item in the inventory. It was called from `read_inv()`, because it is the only place in the program where the information is available. You will also change this location in future chapters as well.

In this project, you will add functionality to your program that allows you to read in the information for the entire inventory by adding a loop to the `read_inv()` function. You still will call the `sell()` and `list_one()` functions from the `read_inv()` function, and you will continue to read in a book number, book price, and the quantity in inventory. Now, however, you will carry out these steps repetitively for each item in the inventory. In future assignments, you will include additional information about each book. Your `read_inv()` function should also write updated data to the output file, outBooks.dat.

You also will write a menu function based on the following requirements:

Menu Letter	Description
L	Lists all of the information in the inventory. This function is a stub—that is, a function that you are not ready to write. You will usually include only one statement in the stub function, which will announce that you are in the function. That statement might be `cout << "In the list_all function." << endl;`.
D	Takes a delivery of books to add to the inventory (this function is also a stub).
R	Produces a daily sales report (this function is also a stub).
Q	Quits the program.

Your menu function should return the choice that the user entered. The return value will allow your `main()` function to call the correct function. The inventory information is stored in the file saved as inBooks.dat in the Chapter5 folder on your Student Disk. Save your program as Ch5-pp1.cpp in the Chapter5 folder.

2. Baseball Simulation

In Chapter 4, you modified the `pitch()` function to select the type of pitch thrown based on a random number. You also wrote a function named `batter_up()` that used the random number generator to determine whether the batter got a hit, strike, ball, or an out. In this project, you will add functionality to your program that provides for playing nine innings. Write a function named `team_play()` that invokes your `pitch()` and `batter_up()` functions. The `team_play()` function will be called twice from your `main()` function for each of the nine innings—once for the White Sox and once for the Tigers. Stay in the `team_play()` function until the team has three outs. You will still be able to announce whether a player got a hit, struck out, popped out, grounded out, flied out, or walked. In future chapters, you will add functionality that enables you to keep score. Save your program as Ch5-pp2.cpp in the Chapter5 folder on your Student Disk.

INDEPENDENT PROJECTS

1. Encryption and Decryption Program

The Careful Credit Card Company has hired you to write a C++ program that encrypts the contents of a file or decrypts the contents of an encrypted file. When you first run your program, choose Encrypt a File from the menu and encrypt the file saved as credit.dat in the Chapter5 folder on your Student Disk. Save the encrypted data in a file named encrypt.dat. Next, choose Decrypt a File from the menu and decrypt the newly created encrypt.dat file. Save the decrypted data as decrypt.dat.

The file contains customers' credit card numbers followed by their last and first names. To encrypt the file, use the following rules:

- Write numeric characters as the numbers 257 through 266.
- Write all other characters as their ASCII value.

Decryption of the file follows the same rules in reverse. When you are finished, save your program as Ch5-ip1.cpp in the Chapter5 folder on your Student Disk.

2. File Compression

Write a C++ program that copies one file into another file and compresses the first file while copying it. Open the file saved as inComp.dat from the Chapter5 folder on your Student Disk; save the compressed version of the same file as outComp.dat. You will use a compression scheme that replaces multiple whitespace characters with a single space character. Whitespace is defined as spaces, tabs, and newlines. A multiple instance of whitespace is defined as two or more whitespace characters appearing in sequence. For example, if three spaces appear as consecutive characters, then replace all three with a single space. If two spaces, two tabs, and one newline character appear in sequence, then replace all of the whitespace characters with a single space. Save your program as Ch5-ip2.cpp in the Chapter5 folder.

Arrays and Strings

Introduction ▶ In this chapter, you will learn how to use, declare, and initialize arrays. You will access array elements and learn about overrunning the bounds of C++ arrays. In addition, you will review how to use arrays to create strings and learn about C++ string-handling functions.

What Is an Array?

An **array** is a group of data items in which every data item has the same data type and is referenced using the same variable name. The data items in an array are stored consecutively in memory. To reference individual data items in an array, you use an **index**. The value of the index is used to calculate an offset into the array. In C++, indexing starts at 0 (zero) and should end with n - 1, where *n* is the number of items stored in the array.

Syntax

▶ char ssn[11];
   int temperatures[7];
   double salaries[200];

Declaring an Array

Before you can use an array in your C++ program, you must declare it. To declare an array, you specify the data type of the items that will be stored in the array, the name of the array, and the number of items that the array can hold.

For example, to create an array named **phone** that can store a maximum of 13 characters, use the following code: `char phone[13];`.

To declare an array of integers named **grades** that uses an integer constant for the size, use the following code:

```
const int MAXSTU = 8;
long grades[MAXSTU];
```

The C++ compiler reserves consecutive memory storage locations for arrays. Thus the compiler will reserve 13 bytes for the **phone** array and 32 bytes for the **grades** array. C++ will keep track of the beginning (or base) address of the arrays. The name of an array without an index translates to the base address of the array. Figure 6-1 shows the storage of the **phone** and **grades** arrays.

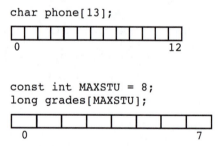

Figure 6-1: Memory allocation for arrays

Exercise

Exercise 6.1 ▶ Write array declarations for each of the following items:

    a. Five ages _____

    b. Five salaries _____

    c. A first name _____

    d. A last name _____

    e. Three initials _____

    f. Ten weights (in ounces) _____

Initializing an Array

You can initialize an array with values when you declare it. Alternatively, you can assign values to an array using assignment statements. To initialize an array when you declare it, use curly braces to surround a comma-delimited list of data items, as shown in Example 6-1.

Example 6·1

```
char name[15] = {'R', 'A', 'Y', 'M', 'O', 'N', 'D', '\0'};
name[0] now contains R
name[6] now contains D
name[7] now contains \0
```

The values in name[8] through name[14] are unknown or initialized with null values, depending on the storage class of the array.

You also can initialize an array without specifying the array's size. Example 6-2 shows the code to initialize an array of integers in this manner.

Example 6·2

```
int grades[] = {95, 92, 91, 75};
```

The size of the grades array is 4 because the array is initialized with four values. The values in grades[0] through grades[3] are 95, 92, 91, and 75, respectively.

Example 6-3 shows the code to initialize an array using assignment statements.

Example 6·3

```
constint MAXSTU = 35;
int grades[MAXSTU];

grades[0] = 95;
grades[1] = 92;
```

You also could use a loop to assign values to all elements in an array, as shown in Example 6-4.

Example 6·4

```
for(i = 0; i < MAXSTU; i++)
    grades[i] = i * 10;
```

Exercise

Exercise 6.2 ▶ On a piece of paper, initialize an array that stores the following information.
    a. The ages 15, 54, 23, 3, and 22
    b. The salaries 25,000.00, 35,000.00, 45,000.00, 55,000.00, and 65,000.00
    c. The last name Thompson
    d. The first name Pamela
    e. The initials JEJ
    f. The weights (in ounces) 56, 94, 32, 8, 12, 45, 78, 99, 102, and 1

Accessing an Array Item

You need to access individual locations in an array when you assign a value to an array element, print its value, change its value, assign the value to another variable, and so forth. In C++, you use integer expressions placed in square brackets to indicate which element in the array should be accessed. This integer expression is the index. Remember that indexing begins at zero in C++.

The code in Example 6-5 initializes an array of integers, copies values from one array to another, changes several values stored in the target array, and prints the values of the source and target arrays.

Example 6-5

```cpp
// Ex6-5.cpp
#include <iostream.h>
int main()
{
  const int MAXNUM = 15;
  int target_array[MAXNUM];
  // Initialize source array.
  int source_array[MAXNUM] = \
    {1,3,5,7,9,11,13,15,17,19,21,23,25,27,29};
  int i;

  // Copy values from source_array to target_array.
  for(i = 0; i < MAXNUM; i++)
    target_array[i] = source_array[i];

  // Assign values to two elements of the target_array.
  target_array[0] = 2;
  target_array[1] = 4;

  // Print values stored in source_array
  // and target_array.
  for(i = 0; i < MAXNUM; i++)
  {
    cout << "Value of source_array[" << i << "] is " \
      << source_array[i];
    cout << "\tValue of target_array[" << i << "] is " \
      << target_array[i] << endl;
  }

  return 0;

}
```

Exercises

Exercise 6.3 ▶

You need to modify the home repair program that you changed in Exercise 5-14 in Chapter 5. Now you will use an array to store the dollar amounts of the home repairs that you want to make. Study the C++ program saved as Ch6-3.cpp in the Chapter6 folder on your Student Disk, and then make the necessary changes. Save the modified program as Ch6-3a.cpp in the Chapter6 folder. Use the prioritized data from Exercise 5-14 to run this program.

Exercise 6.4 ▶

You have written a C++ program that finds the minimum and maximum values stored in an array. Your program, however, does not produce the correct results. Study the C++ program saved as Ch6-4.cpp in the Chapter6 folder on your Student Disk, make the necessary changes, and then save the debugged version as Ch6-4a.cpp in the Chapter6 folder.

Exercise 6.5 ▶

Your school's basketball coach has asked you to write a C++ program that will let him enter and save the final score for each of the 30 games his team plays during a season. This program should print the high point score, the low point score, and the average number of points scored by the team. Save your program as Ch6-5a.cpp in the Chapter6 folder on your Student Disk. The total points for the 30 games are stored in the file named bball.dat in the Chapter6 folder.

Overrunning an Array

C++ does not perform range checking. As a C++ programmer, it is your responsibility to ensure that the index values used to access array elements are within the legal range. If you overrun the bounds of an array, the value stored at that memory location is read or overwritten. You also could cause your program to abort by referencing an out-of-bounds memory location. In Example 6-6, the program overruns the bounds of an array named `age_array`.

Example 6-6

```
// Ex6-6.cpp
#include <iostream.h>
int main()
{
  const int MAXNUM = 5;
  // Compiler reserves 10 bytes of memory for age_array.
  short age_array[MAXNUM];
  // Compiler reserves next 2 bytes for my_age.
  short my_age;
  int i;

  my_age = 29;    // Assign 29 to my_age.
  for(i = 0; i <= MAXNUM; i++)
    age_array[i] = i + 10;
  // Last iteration assigns 15 to my_age
  // because index[5] is out of range
  // and my_age is stored at the 2 bytes
  // after age_array.

  cout << "My age is " << my_age << endl;
  for(i = 0 ; i <= MAXNUM; i++)
    cout << "age_array[" << i << "] is " \
      << age_array[i] << endl;

  return 0

}
```

The output of this program is:

```
My age is 15
age_array[0] is 10
age_array[1] is 11
age_array[2] is 12
age_array[3] is 13
age_array[4] is 14
age_array[5] is 15
```

Some compilers reserve storage differently, so your output might be different from the results shown in this example. In any case, you should avoid overrunning arrays in C++ programs.

Figure 6-2 shows the last iteration of the loop that assigned values to the `age_array`. It went beyond the bounds of the array and assigned the value 15 in the memory location associated with the variable named `my_age`. When the program prints the value of `my_age`, the value is 15. When it prints the value of `age_array[5]`, however, its value is also 15.

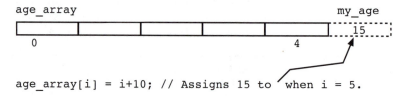

Figure 6-2: Overrunning the bounds of an array

Exercise

Exercise 6.6 ▶

The C++ program saved as Ch6-6.cpp in the Chapter6 folder on your Student Disk reads 26 test scores into an array and finds the highest, lowest, and average of the 26 scores. The program does not compile, so you are not sure that it will produce the correct output. Find and correct the syntax errors, and then run the program to ensure that it produces the correct output. If the output still contains errors, find and correct the logic errors. Save your corrected program as Ch6-6a.cpp in the Chapter6 folder.

Parallel Arrays

You use a **parallel array** to store values in multiple arrays so as to maintain a relationship between the items. Figure 6-3 shows that the student ID number stored in `stu_id[0]` and the grade stored in `grades[0]` are related—student 56 received a grade of 99. This relationship is established by using the same index value when accessing each array. Note that the programmer must maintain this relationship—C++ does not create or maintain the relationship.

```
int stu_id[4];
```

56	22	11	44
0			3

```
int grades[4];
```

99	77	88	55
0			3

Figure 6-3: Parallel arrays

Exercises

Exercise 6.7 ▶

You wrote a program for your meteorology class that reads and stores the high and low temperatures for each day in March. After you enter all of your temperature data, your program allows you to enter a date in March and then prints the high and low temperatures for that day. Modify this program so that it also prints the low and high temperatures for the entire month. The current program is saved as Ch6-7.cpp in the Chapter6 folder on your Student Disk. Study it and then make the necessary changes. Save the modified program as Ch6-7a.cpp in the Chapter6 folder.

Exercise 6.8 ▶

You wrote a program that stores information about your treadmill workouts during any given month. The program allows you to enter the date as an integer (1 through 31), the number of calories burned in the workout, the number of miles walked, and your walking speed. If you do not enter values for a date, your program should record 0 (zero) values for the number of calories, miles, and speed. At the end of the month, you can choose an option from the program's menu to calculate monthly totals and averages. Although your program compiles, it does not produce the correct output. Find and correct the errors. The program is saved as Ch6-8.cpp in the Chapter6 folder on your Student Disk. Save the corrected program as Ch6-8a.cpp in the Chapter6 folder.

Exercise 6.9 ▶

You need to write a C++ program that tracks the number of calories and the number of fat grams per serving for 10 food products. The food products have been assigned the numbers 0 through 9 to preserve their anonymity. The calorie and fat gram data are found in the file named food.dat in the Chapter6 folder on your Student Disk. The data for each product appears on a separate line in the following format:

calories

fat grams

The data on the first two lines apply to food product number 0. Read the data into parallel arrays and then print the product number, calories, and fat grams for the food product with the fewest calories. Next, print the product number, calories, and fat grams for the food product with the fewest fat grams. Save your program as Ch6-9a.cpp in the Chapter6 folder.

Character Arrays and Strings

Because C++ does not provide a string data type, you must use an array of characters to store a string. In C++, strings are terminated with the null character or null byte, '\0'. When you declare a character array for a string, you must include an extra space for the '\0' at the end of the string. Example 6-7 shows two methods that initialize an array to store a name as a string. Because the `firstname` array is initialized with a string constant, C++ will automatically add the '\0' at the end of the string. The `lastname` array is initialized character-by-character. Therefore, the programmer must assign the '\0' explicitly.

Example 6-7

```
char firstname[8] = "Timothy";
char lastname[9];
lastname[0] = 'M';
lastname[1] = 'o';
lastname[2] = 'r';
lastname[3] = 'i';
lastname[4] = 'a';
```

```
lastname[5] = 'r';
lastname[6] = 't';
lastname[7] = 'y';
lastname[8] = '\0';
```

Figure 6-4 shows the contents of the `firstname` and `lastname` arrays.

firstname

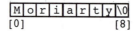

[0]   [7]

lastname

M o r i a r t y \0
[0]   [8]

Figure 6-4: Contents of the `firstname` and `lastname` arrays

Many C++ functions and methods were written to expect the `'\0'` because this character offered the only way to determine where the string ended. For example, you can use the insertion and extraction operators with `cin` and `cout` to read and write strings, as shown in Example 6-8.

Example 6-8

```
const int NAME_LEN = 15;
// Allocates storage for 15 characters.
char firstname[NAME_LEN];
// Reads and stores user input as a string.
cin >> firstname;
// Prints the string stored in firstname.
cout << firstname
```

You will learn about additional functions that are written to deal with strings in the next section.

Exercises

Exercise 6.10 ▶

MODIFY

The C++ program saved as Ch6-10.cpp in the Chapter6 folder on your Student Disk allows you to enter a character and then prints that character's ASCII value. Modify this program so that you can enter up to 79 characters, store them as a string, and then print each character's ASCII value. Save your new program as Ch6-10a.cpp in the Chapter6 folder.

Exercise 6.11 ▶

DEBUG

The C++ program saved as Ch6-11.cpp in the Chapter6 folder on your Student Disk reads a string and then prints it backward. Although the program compiles, it does not produce the correct output. Study the program, and then fix the errors. Save the corrected program as Ch6-11a.cpp in the Chapter6 folder.

Exercise 6.12 ▶

DEVELOP

Write a C++ program that reads characters entered at the keyboard and counts the number of vowels. The program should continue to read characters until the user types the EOF character. The EOF character is Ctrl + Z (for Windows or DOS) or Ctrl + D (for UNIX). The program should report the total number of characters and vowels read. Save your program as Ch6-12a.cpp in the Chapter6 folder on your Student Disk.

String I/O

You use the get( ) function with cin or an opened file to input string data. Two arguments are required. The first argument is a string variable that represents the storage location for the read characters. The second argument is an integer expression that represents the maximum number of characters to read. The get( ) function will read characters into the string variable until it reads one less than the specified number of characters or it reads a newline character ('\n'). The newline character is neither stored as part of the string nor extracted from the input stream. The get( ) function appends a null character ('\0') to the string. The function does not skip leading whitespace characters.

The C++ code in Example 6-9 reads a maximum of 80 characters into the character array named input_line and appends a null character ('\0').

Example 6-9
```
const int LINE_LEN = 81;
char input_line[LINE_LEN];
cin.get(input_line, LINE_LEN);
```

You can use the getline( ) function with cin or an opened file to input string data. Using the getline( ) function is similar to using the get( ) function, except that the newline character ('\n') is extracted from the input stream when it is read. The newline character is not stored in the array, however. In Example 6-10, a getline( ) function reads a maximum of 80 characters into the array named input_line or stops when it reads the newline character. The newline character is extracted from the input stream.

Example 6-10
```
const int LINE_LEN = 81;
char input_line[LINE_LEN];
cin.getline(input_line, LINE_LEN);
```

You can use a third argument with the get( ) and getline( ) functions to specify the delimiter character. The default is the newline character ('\n'). If this third argument is included, the get( ) and getline( ) functions will continue to read characters until they read either the specified number of characters or the specified delimiter. In Example 6-11, the getline( ) function reads a maximum of 80 characters or stops when it reads a space.

Example 6-11
```
const int LINE_LEN = 81;
char input_line[LINE_LEN];
cin.getline(input_line, LINE_LEN, ' ');
```

The ignore( ) function reads and discards up to a specified number of characters. This function expects two arguments: the number of characters to extract and discard, and the delimiter character. The default delimiter is EOF. In Example 6-12, the ignore( ) function skips up to 100 characters or stops when it reads a newline character ('\n'). The delimiter character is extracted from the input stream.

Example 6-12
```
cin.ignore(100, '\n');
```

Exercises

Exercise 6.13 ▶

The C++ program saved as Ch6-13.cpp in the Chapter6 folder on your Student Disk copies one file to another file. It opens two files—one to read from and one to write to. In its current form, the program reads the file and writes the file one character at a time. Modify this program to read and write one line at a time. Save your modified program as Ch6-13a.cpp in the Chapter6 folder.

Exercise 6.14 ▶

Your address book is stored as address.dat in the Chapter6 folder on your Student Disk. You wrote a C++ program that reads in the contents of the address book file and then prints each person's name, address, telephone number, and e-mail address. This program, which is saved as Ch6-14.cpp in the Chapter6 folder on your Student Disk, does not work correctly. Find and fix the errors, and then save the corrected program as Ch6-14a.cpp in the Chapter6 folder.

Exercise 6.15 ▶

Charlene Ramirez, the owner of the Value Video Store, has asked you to write a C++ program that lets her enter a video's unique ID number. The program should then respond with the number of copies of the video with that ID number currently in inventory. The inventory is saved as video.dat in the Chapter6 folder. In this file, data are stored in a format where the video ID number appears on one line and the number of copies follows on the next line. For example:

16728

12

16872

13

17320

34

The inventory can hold a maximum of 100 videos. Save your program as Ch6-15a.cpp in the Chapter6 folder.

Character- and String-Handling Functions

C++ provides several functions that allow you to test and manipulate character data. The function prototypes are found in the header file named `ctype.h`. Remember to add the line `#include <ctype.h>` in programs that use these functions.

Figure 6-5 lists and describes each of these functions. Each function expects one integer argument—the ASCII value of the character to be tested. Each function returns a non-zero value (true) if the condition tested is true and 0 (false) if the condition tested is false.

Function	Description
`int isalnum(int c);`	Alphanumeric ('A'–'Z', 'a'–'z', or '0'–'9')
`int isalpha(int c);`	Letter ('A'–'Z' or 'a'–'z')
`int iscntrl(int c);`	Control character (0x00–0x1F or 0x7F)
`int isdigit(int c);`	Digit ('0'–'9')
`int isgraph(int c);`	Printable character except space (' ')
`int islower(int c);`	Lowercase letter ('a'–'z')
`int isprint(int c);`	Printable character (0x20–0x7E)
`int ispunct(int c);`	Punctuation character
`int isspace(int c);`	Whitespace character (tab, space, newline)
`int isupper(int c);`	Uppercase letter ('A'–'Z')
`int isxdigit(int c);`	Hexadecimal digit ('A'–'F','a'–'f', or '0'–'9')

Figure 6-5: Character-handling functions

The functions shown in Figure 6-6 expect one integer argument—the ASCII value of the character to be converted. Both functions return an integer—the ASCII value of the converted character.

Function	Description
`int tolower(int c);`	Converts c to lowercase if appropriate
`int toupper(int c);`	Converts c to uppercase if appropriate

Figure 6-6: Character conversion functions

Example 6-13 shows how to use several of these functions.

Example 6-13

```cpp
// Ex6-13.cpp
#include <iostream.h>
#include <ctype.h>

int main()
{
  const int MAX_NAME = 15;
  char name[MAX_NAME];
  int i;

  cout << "Enter your first name: ";
  cin >> name;
```

```
        if(islower(name[0]))  // If first letter is lowercase
            // Convert to uppercase
            name[0] = toupper(name[0]);

        for(i = 1; i < MAX_NAME; i++)
          if(isupper(name[i]))  // If character is uppercase
            // Convert to lowercase
            name[i] = tolower(name[i]);

        cout << "Your first name is " << name << endl;

        return 0;

    }
```

If the program's input is joANN, then the program's output is:

```
Your first name is Joann.
```

The C++ functions shown in Figure 6-7 help process strings. Remember to add the line #include <string.h> in any program that uses these string functions. These functions expect arguments that are null-terminated strings, which means that the string arguments to these functions are expected to contain a null character ('\0') to mark the end of the string. The declarations are shown as they appear in string.h. Notice the arguments are of type char*. This is an alternative method used to specify an array of characters. You will learn more about this in Chapter 7.

String and Description

```
char* strcpy(char* string1, const char* string2);
```
Copies string2 to string1, stopping after the null character is copied, and then returns string1.

```
char* strncpy(char* string1, const char* string2, size_t count);
```
Same as strcpy but copies exactly count characters.

```
int strcmp(const char* string1, const char* string2);
```
Returns a value less than, equal to, or greater than 0, if string1 is less than, equal to, or greater than string2, respectively.

```
int strncmp(const char* string1, const char* string2, size_t count);
```
Same as strcmp but compares no more than count characters.

```
size_t strlen(const char* string);
```
Returns the number of characters in string up to, but not including, '\0'.

```
char* strcat(char* string1, const char* string2);
```
Appends string2 to string1 and returns string1.

```
char* strncat(char* string1, const char* string2, size_t count);
```
Same as strcat but appends at most count characters.

Figure 6-7: String-handling functions

Example 6-14 shows how to use several of these functions.

Example 6-14

```cpp
// Ex6-14.cpp
#include <string.h>
#include <iostream.h>
const int STRING_LEN = 20;
int main()
{
  char string1[] = "How now brown Cow.";
  char string2[] = "How now brown cow.";
  char tmp[STRING_LEN];
  int result;

  cout << "Compare first 10 characters of strings: " \
    << endl << string1 << endl << string2 << endl;

  // Compares first 10 characters only.
  result = strncmp(string1, string2, 10);
  if(result > 0)
    strcpy(tmp, "greater than");
  else if(result < 0)
    strcpy(tmp, "less than");
  else
    strcpy(tmp, "equal to");

  cout << "Result: string1 is " << tmp << " string 2" \
    << endl << endl;

  cout << "Compare all characters of strings: " << endl \
    << string1 << endl << string2 << endl;

  // Compares all characters in two strings.
  result = strcmp(string1, string2);
  if(result > 0)
    strcpy(tmp, "greater than");
  else if(result < 0)
    strcpy(tmp, "less than");
  else
    strcpy(tmp, "equal to");

  cout << "Result: string1 is " << tmp \
    << " string 2" << endl << endl;

  return 0;
}
```

The output of this program is:
```
Compare first 10 characters of strings:
How now brown Cow.
How now brown cow.
Result: string1 is equal to string 2
```

```
Compare all characters of strings:
How now brown Cow.
How now brown cow.
Result: string1 is less than string 2
```

Exercises

Exercise 6.16 ▶

M O D I F Y

The C++ program saved as Ch6-16.cpp in the Chapter6 folder on your Student Disk counts the number of lowercase letters and the total number of characters in a file. Modify the program so that it also counts the number of uppercase letters, numeric characters, whitespace characters, and punctuation characters in the file. Save your modified program as Ch6-16a.cpp in the Chapter6 folder.

Exercise 6.17 ▶

D E B U G

The C++ program saved as Ch6-17.cpp in the Chapter6 folder on your Student Disk verifies a user's login ID and password. Login IDs and passwords are stored in a file named lookup.dat in the Chapter6 folder on your Student Disk. The program interactively asks a user for his or her login ID and password. It then looks up the ID and password in the lookup.dat file to verify that the user entered the correct information. If the login and password match the values stored in the file, the program prints a message informing the user that the login was successful. If the ID and password do not match the values stored in the file, it prints a message informing the user that the login failed. This program is not working correctly, however, because users with incorrect logins and passwords are allowed to log in. Find and fix the errors, and then save the corrected program as Ch6-17a.cpp in the Chapter6 folder.

Exercise 6.18 ▶

D E V E L O P

Rewrite the program described in Exercise 6-12 using functions found in `ctype.h`. Save your program as Ch6-18a.cpp in the Chapter6 folder on your Student Disk.

Using a Multidimensional Array

A **multidimensional array** stores data that require multiple dimensions to represent them. For example, to store monthly sales data for a chain-store operation with 50 stores nationwide, you could use a two-dimensional array—one dimension representing sales data for each of the 12 months and a second dimension representing the sales data for each of the 50 stores. A multidimensional array requires the use of more than one index. You can think of a two-dimensional array as a table of values stored in rows and columns.

Figure 6-8 shows the two-dimensional array used to store 12 months of sales data for 50 stores. It requires you to use two indexes—one for the rows in the table and the other for the columns in the table.

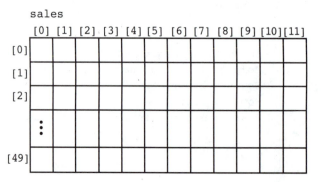

Figure 6-8: Two-dimensional array

In Example 6-15, a two-dimensional array named sales is declared. Each row in this array will store the monthly sales data for one of the 50 stores. Each column will represent one month's sales total for each of the 50 stores.

Example 6-15

```
const int NUM_STORES = 50;
const int NUM_MONTHS = 12;
double sales[NUM_STORES][NUM_MONTHS];
```

Example 6-16 illustrates that you need two indexes to access the elements of the two-dimensional array.

Example 6-16

```
const int NUM_STORES = 50;
const int NUM_MONTHS = 12;
double sales[NUM_STORES][NUM_MONTHS];
int store_num, month_num;

store_num = 0;
month_num = 0;
sales[store_num][month_num] = 1275.00;
```

Example 6-17 shows how to use nested loops to access each item stored in a multidimensional array.

Example 6-17

```cpp
// Ex6-17.cpp
#include <iostream.h>
int main()
{
  const int NUM_STORES = 50;
  const int NUM_MONTHS = 12;
  double sales[NUM_STORES][NUM_MONTHS];
  int store, month;

  for(store = 0; store < NUM_STORES; store++)
  {
    for(month = 0; month < NUM_MONTHS; month++)
    {
      cout << "Enter a sales total for Store Number " \
        << store + 1;
      cout << " Month Number " << month + 1<< ":";
      cin >> sales[store][month];
    }
  }
  for(store = 0; store < NUM_STORES; store++)
  {
    for(month = 0; month < NUM_MONTHS; month++)
    {
      cout << "Sales for Store Number " << store + 1;
      cout << " during Month Number " << month + 1 << " is ";
      cout << sales[store][month] << endl;
    }
  }
  return 0;
}
```

Example 6-18 shows the code to initialize a multidimensional array.

Example 6-18

```
const int NUM_ROWS = 2;
const int NUM_COLS = 3;
int num_array[NUM_ROWS][NUM_COLS] = {{1,2,3}, {3,2,1}};
```

Example 6-19 shows how to declare a three-dimensional array.

Example 6-19

```
const int NUM_ROWS = 22;
const int NUM_SEATS = 15;
const int NUM_LEVELS = 2;
int arena[NUM_ROWS][NUM_SEATS][NUM_LEVELS];
```

The array declared in Example 6-19 requires three indexes and three loops to access the values stored in the array.

Example 6-20 shows how to declare an *n*-dimensional array.

Example 6-20

```
int multi_array[3][5]…[n];
```

The array declared in Example 6-20 requires *n* indexes and *n* loops to access the values stored in the array.

Exercises

Exercise 6.19 ▶

MODIFY

Modify the program saved as Ch6-19.cpp in the Chapter6 folder on your Student Disk to find the minimum and maximum values stored in a two-dimensional array. The array should have three rows and four columns. Row 1 should contain the values 66, 22, -1, and 0. Row 2 should contain the values 72, 11, -3, and 99. Row 3 should contain the values 26, 11, 5, and 52. Save the modified program as Ch6-19a.cpp in the Chapter6 folder.

Exercise 6.20 ▶

DEBUG

You are developing a program that prints the board for an intermediate-level minesweeper game. For now, you will show only the positions of the mines. In an intermediate-level game, the board contains 16 rows, 16 columns, and 40 mines. You want to show the mines by printing the letter *M* in a square on the board and printing a dash in squares without mines. The program is almost working, but a few problems persist. Find and fix the errors in the program saved as Ch6-20.cpp in the Chapter6 folder on your Student Disk, and then save the corrected program as Ch6-20a.cpp.

Exercise 6.21 ▶

DEVELOP

Freda Kozinski of the Build-Rite Manufacturing Company has asked you to write a C++ program that calculates shipping charges for orders. All orders are charged a basic shipping rate of $20.00, plus an additional rate based on the quantity of items shipped and the destination. The shipping rates are as follows:

Quantity	Region 1	Region 2	Region 3	Region 4	Region 5
1	1.00	2.00	3.00	4.00	5.00
2	2.00	4.00	6.00	8.00	10.00
3	2.50	4.50	6.50	8.50	10.50
4	3.00	5.00	7.00	9.00	11.00
5	3.25	5.25	7.25	9.25	11.25
More than 5	3.50	5.50	7.50	9.50	11.50

Your program should prompt the user to enter the quantity of items and the destination shipping region, and then calculate a shipping rate. Use a two-dimensional array in your solution. Save your work as Ch6-21a.cpp in the Chapter6 folder on your Student Disk.

Passing Arrays to Functions

When a function invocation includes the name of an array, the beginning memory address of the array is passed by value. Although you cannot change the beginning memory address of the array in the function, you can access the values stored in the array. In the function declaration and function definition, you do not specify the size of the array; rather, you use empty square brackets to indicate an array without the size specified. In Example 6-21, the program copies the contents of one array into a second array and passes these arrays to functions.

Example 6-21

```
// Ex6-21.cpp
#include <iostream.h>
#include <string.h>
const int SIZE = 25;

void copy_array(char[], char[]);

int main()
{
  char target[SIZE], source[SIZE];

  strcpy(source, "Hello world");
  // Invoke the function with the name
  // of the target and source arrays.
  copy_array(target,source);
  cout << source << endl;
  cout << target << endl;

  return 0;

}
// Function definition; arguments declared as arrays.
void copy_array(char to_array[], char from_array[])
```

```
{
  int k;
  for(k = 0;from_array[k] != '\0'; k++)
      to_array[k] = from_array[k];
  to_array[k] = '\0'; // Be sure to copy the '\0'
}
```

The output of this program is:
```
Hello world
Hello world
```

You also can pass multidimensional arrays to C++ functions. When passing a multidimensional array, use the name of the array without an index in the function call. In the function declaration and function definition, you do not need to specify the size of the first dimension. You must, however, specify all other dimensions.

Exercises

Exercise 6.22 ▶

M O D I F Y

The C++ program saved as Ch6-22.cpp in the Chapter6 folder on your Student Disk accepts names interactively from the user and then calls a function to change all characters in the name to uppercase letters. Modify this program to change only the first letter of each name to uppercase and all other characters to lowercase. Save your modified program as Ch6-22a.cpp in the Chapter6 folder.

Exercise 6.23 ▶

D E B U G

The C++ program saved as Ch6-23.cpp in the Chapter6 folder on your Student Disk calls a function that initializes an array of integers to all zeroes. This array is then passed to the calling function. This program does not compile, so you do not know whether it works correctly. Find and fix the errors so that it runs correctly, and then save the corrected program as Ch6-23a.cpp in the Chapter6 folder.

Exercise 6.24 ▶

D E V E L O P

Jane Goode, the owner of the Goodebody Health Food Store, has asked you to write a C++ program that calls a function to read in the names of products and their prices from a file named health.dat, which is saved in the Chapter6 folder on your Student Disk. The names will be stored in one array and their prices will be stored in a second array. There is a maximum of 50 products. After the items have been read in from the file, your program should call another function to print the names of the products and their prices to the screen. Save your program as Ch6-24a.cpp in the Chapter6 folder.

Sort Algorithms

An **algorithm** is a plan for solving a problem. There are many algorithms to sort data, which you can use on data stored in an array. The **bubble sort** is a sort algorithm that "bubbles" up lighter (smaller) values to the top or beginning of the list. Heavier (larger) values sink to the bottom or end of the list.

The bubble sort is logically simple but not very efficient. If the list contains n values, the bubble sort will make $n - 1$ passes over the list. During each pass, it examines successive overlapped pairs and exchanges those values that are out of order. After one pass, the lightest (smallest) value floats to the top. On the second pass, you can ignore the first value in the list because it is in its proper position. On the third pass, you do not have to worry about the first and second values in the list, because they are positioned correctly. Thus, in each subsequent pass, you reduce the number of items to be compared, and possibly swapped, by one. The program in Example 6-22 uses a bubble sort to reorder a list of integers.

Example 6-22

```cpp
// Ex6-22.cpp
#include <iostream.h>

void bubble(int[], int);

int main()
{
  const int NUM_ELEMENTS = 8;
  int numbers[NUM_ELEMENTS] = {15,22,105,0,11,-5,62,88};
  int j;

  cout << "Before the bubble sort." << endl << endl;

  // Prints all values in the array.
  for(j = 0; j < NUM_ELEMENTS; j++)
    cout << "Value of numbers[" << j << "] is " \
      << numbers[j] << endl;
    // Invoke bubble sort.
  bubble(numbers, NUM_ELEMENTS);

  cout << endl << endl << "After the bubble sort." << endl << endl;

  // Print values in array.
  // This time they should be in sorted order.
  for(j = 0; j < NUM_ELEMENTS; j++)
    cout << "Value of numbers[" << j << "] is " \
      << numbers[j] << endl;

  return 0;

}
void bubble (int num_array[], int num)
{
  int j, k, temp;

  for(j=0; j < num - 1; j++)  // n - 1 passes
  {
    // Each pass runs one fewer than the preceding pass.
    for(k = num - 1; j < k; k--)
    {
      if(num_array[k-1] > num_array[k])
      {
        temp = num_array[k-1];
        num_array[k-1] = num_array[k];
        num_array[k] = temp;
      }
    }
  }
}
```

The output of this program before the bubble sort is:
```
Value of numbers[0] is 15
Value of numbers[1] is 22
Value of numbers[2] is 105
Value of numbers[3] is 0
```

```
Value of numbers[4] is 11
Value of numbers[5] is -5
Value of numbers[6] is 62
Value of numbers[7] is 88
```

The output of this program after the bubble sort is:

```
Value of numbers[0] is -5
Value of numbers[1] is 0
Value of numbers[2] is 11
Value of numbers[3] is 15
Value of numbers[4] is 22
Value of numbers[5] is 62
Value of numbers[6] is 88
Value of numbers[7] is 105
```

Exercises

Exercise 6.25 ▶

The C++ program saved as Ch6-25.cpp in the Chapter6 folder on your Student Disk reads a file named ids.dat (stored in the Chapter6 folder) that contains product ID numbers and prices. The program reads the data into two arrays—one for the product ID numbers and the other for their prices. It then calls a bubble sort to sort the array holding the product ID numbers and, at the same time, moves the values stored in the prices array so that the prices remain associated with the correct item. Modify this program so that it reads product names and prices (instead of product ID numbers and prices) from a file named health.dat in the Chapter6 folder. The modified program should sort on the product name. As in the original program, the prices should be moved to the correct location in the prices array. Save the modified program as Ch6-25a.cpp in the Chapter6 folder.

Exercise 6.26 ▶

The C++ program saved as Ch6-26.cpp in the Chapter6 folder on your Student Disk reads in a maximum of 50 English words, sorts them using a bubble sort, and then prints them. The English words are found in a file named engl.dat in the Chapter6 folder. The program does not compile, so you do not know whether it works correctly. Find and fix the syntax errors, and then make sure the program runs correctly. Save your corrected program as Ch6-26a.cpp in the Chapter6 folder.

Exercise 6.27 ▶

Melvin Singer, the owner of Mel's Music Store, has asked you to write a C++ program that reads in his inventory and prints all CD titles in alphabetical order. Do not print anything except the CD titles. The inventory list is found in a file named mel.dat in the Chapter6 folder on your Student Disk. The data are stored in the following format:

Name_of_Recording Type_of_Recording

For example:

Highway 61 CD

The Singles Collection CD

Highway 61 Album

Live at Newport CD

Blue Aconite CD

Round of Blues CD

Touch Me Fall CD

Born in the USA Album

Mel's inventory contains a maximum of 100 titles. Save your program as Ch6-27a.cpp in the Chapter6 folder.

Search Algorithms

After sorting a list, you can use algorithms to write a C++ function that searches for data stored in the sorted list. You can use a **binary search** to search for items stored in an array. The binary search algorithm is very efficient, especially compared with a sequential search, which begins with the first element in the list and continues to search sequentially until it finds the desired item.

The binary search algorithm divides the list in half. It then decides which half of the list to continue searching by comparing the item in the middle of the list with the desired item. It discards the other half of the list. The algorithm continues to divide the remaining list in half and discard the other half until the list consists of one item—the item for which you are searching. If this item is not the desired item, then this item is not in the list.

The program in Example 6-23 uses a binary search to locate a value in a list of integers.

Example 6-23

```cpp
// Ex6-23.cpp
#include <iostream.h>

void bubble(int[], int);
int bin_search(int[], int, int);
const int FALSE = 0;
const int TRUE = 1;

int main()
{
  const int NUM_ELEMENTS = 8;
  int numbers[NUM_ELEMENTS] = {15,22,105,0,11,-5,62,88};
  int item;
  int index;

  // Sort the list of integers.
  bubble(numbers, NUM_ELEMENTS);

  cout << "Enter the value to find in the list: ";
  cin >> item;

  // Invoke bin_search to find the item input by the user.
  index = bin_search(numbers, item, NUM_ELEMENTS);

  if(index < NUM_ELEMENTS)

    cout << item << " was located at index position " \
      << index << " in the numbers array." << endl;
  else
    cout << item \
      << " was not found in the numbers array." << endl;

  return 0;

}
```

```
int bin_search(int num_array[], int item, int num)
{
  int beginning = 0;
  int end = num - 1;
  int middle;
  int location;
  int found;

  found = FALSE;
  // Stay in loop until item is found
  // or list has been divided in two
  // the maximum number of times.
  while(end >= beginning && !found)
  {
    // Find the middle of the list.
    middle = (beginning + end) / 2;
    // Decide which half of the list to search.
    if(item < num_array[middle])
      // Discard the last half of the list.
      end = middle - 1;
    else if(item > num_array[middle])
      // Discard the first half of the list.
      beginning = middle + 1;
    else
      found = TRUE;
  }
  if(found == TRUE)
    location = middle;
  else
    location = num;
  return location;
}

void bubble(int num_array[], int num)
{
  int j, k, temp;

  for(j=0; j < num - 1; j++)  // n - 1 passes
  {
    // Each pass runs one fewer than the preceding pass.
    for(k = num - 1; j < k; k--)
    {
      if(num_array[k-1] > num_array[k])
      {
        temp = num_array[k-1];
        num_array[k-1] = num_array[k];
        num_array[k] = temp;
      }
    }
  }
}
```

Exercises

Exercise 6.28 ▶

M O D I F Y

In Exercise 6-25, you modified a C++ program so that it sorted product names. Modify this program again to search through the list for a particular product name. When the program finds a product name in the list, it should print the name and the price. If the name does not appear in the list, it should print a message telling the user that the product was not found. The program to modify is saved as Ch6-28.cpp in the Chapter6 folder on your Student Disk. Save your modified program as Ch6-28a.cpp.

Exercise 6.29 ▶

D E B U G

The C++ program saved as Ch6-29.cpp in the Chapter6 folder on your Student Disk reads in a list of TV programs, the channels on which they will be broadcast, the times they will appear (Central Standard Time), and the day of the week they will appear. This information is saved as tv.dat in the Chapter6 folder on your Student Disk. The program also sorts the TV program names alphabetically (using a bubble sort). A user can enter the name of a TV program and your program will search the alphabetically sorted list of TV program names. If the TV program is found in the list, the name, channel, and time are printed. If it is not found, a message informs the user that the program could not be found. Because this program does not compile, you do not know whether it works correctly. Find and fix the syntax errors, and then make sure the program runs correctly. If it does not run correctly, find and fix the logic errors. Save the corrected program as Ch6-29a.cpp in the Chapter6 folder.

Exercise 6.30 ▶

D E V E L O P

Write a C++ program that allows you to read in an English-French dictionary into two arrays—one for English words and one for French words. The dictionary data are stored in a file named dict.dat in the Chapter6 folder on your Student Disk. Move the English words until they are sorted alphabetically and also move the associated French words to corresponding locations in the parallel array. Once sorted, your program should allow a user to look up an English word and then print its French equivalent. Your dictionary should be able to store a maximum of 50 English and French words. Save your program as Ch6-30a.cpp in the Chapter6 folder.

S U M M A R Y

- An array is a group of data items that have the same data type. An array is given a name, and the individual elements of the array are then referenced using the array name and an index. Arrays must be declared before you can use them in a C++ program.

- The array declaration includes the data type and number of elements.

- You can initialize an array in a C++ program.

- You should take care not to overrun the bounds of a C++ array.

- Parallel arrays are used to maintain a relationship between data items stored in multiple arrays.

- C++ does not provide a string data type. The programmer must create strings by using a character array and adding the '\0' as the last character in the string.

- You can use the insertion operator (<<) and the extraction operator (>>) with string variables. You also can use the `get()` and `getline()` functions for string input.

- The `ignore()` function is used to read and discard characters.

- Many system-supplied functions are available to facilitate character handling and string handling. You must `#include <ctype.h>` to use the character-handling functions, and you must `#include <string.h>` to use the string-handling functions.

- You can use multidimensional arrays in C++ programs.

- Arrays can be passed to functions.

- Many sort algorithms are available to sort data stored in arrays, including the bubble sort.

- Many search algorithms are available to search for a data item stored in a sorted array, including the binary search.

PROGRESSIVE PROJECTS

1. Books and More

In Chapter 5, you added a function to read in some of the data from the inventory file and a menu function that allows the user to choose the action that your program should perform. In this assignment, you will modify the `read_inv()` function so that it reads in all of the inventory data. Review the contents and format of the file saved as inBooks.dat in the Chapter6 folder on your Student Disk; it now contains more data than in the previous projects. The data file contains the following information for each book: title, author's last name, author's first name, price, publisher, ISBN, copyright date, quantity on hand, and status. You should declare enough parallel arrays in the `main()` function to store the data you read in from inBooks.dat. You will need one additional array to store the number of books sold in one day.

Now that you are able to pass arguments—including arrays—to functions, you should pass the parallel arrays to the `read_inv()` function and any other functions in this project that need the inventory data stored in these arrays.

The `read_inv()` function needs to return an integer. This integer will represent the number of items read in from the inventory file.

After you read in the data from inBooks.dat and store this data in parallel arrays, you should sort on the titles of the books (alphabetically). All other data should be moved to appropriate locations in the other arrays.

After sorting, you should display your menu. Add menu choices for listing the entire inventory, listing one item from the inventory, selling an item from the inventory, and saving the modified inventory data. If a book is out of print (status equals zero) and has a quantity on hand equal to zero, then do not save the book's data to the inventory file. You should also write these functions. All of these functions now should be called from your `main()` function.

A user should now be able to choose one of the following options from the menu:

Menu Item	Description
L	Lists all of the information in the inventory
O	Lists information about one item in the inventory
S	Sells an item from the inventory (subtract from the quantity on hand)
D	Takes a delivery of books to add to the inventory (this function is still a stub)
R	Produces a daily sales report (this function is still a stub)
Q	Quits the program and saves the inventory to the inBooks.dat file

Your menu function should return the choice made by the user, enabling the correct function to be called from your `main()` function. You should pass the appropriate information to these functions.

In future assignments, you will improve the storage methods for your data. You also will write a function to take a delivery of new books as well as a function that prints a daily sales report for the bookstore.

Save your program as Ch6-pp1.cpp in the Chapter6 folder on your Student Disk.

2. Baseball Simulation

In Chapter 5, you added functionality to the baseball simulation project that lets the user play nine innings of baseball, allows both teams to play, determines the types of pitches, and determines the outcome of a batter's time at bat. In this assignment, you will write a function named `read_roster()` that reads the players and their positions into parallel arrays. The roster data are stored in files named team1.dat and team2.dat in the Chapter6 folder on your Student Disk. You will also write a function named `announce_roster()` that announces the players and their positions by printing them to the screen.

In future assignments, you will improve the storage methods for your data and have your program keep score.

Save your program as Ch6-pp2.cpp in the Chapter6 folder on your Student Disk.

INDEPENDENT PROJECTS

1. Hangman

In this project, you will write a Hangman game. The program should read a phrase from a file named wheel.dat that is saved in the Chapter6 folder on your Student Disk. The characters in the phrase should be displayed as underscores, with spaces separating words. For example, if the phrase is "COME AND GET IT", the following series of underscores should display on the user's screen:

_ _ _ _   _ _ _   _ _ _   _ _

As a user guesses letters, the program should display the actual correct letters instead of the underscores. It also should display the number of guesses. The user should be able to continue trying letters until he or she guesses the correct word. He or she should be able to play multiple games and quit the game at any time.

Save your program as Ch6-ip1.cpp in the Chapter6 folder on your Student Disk.

2. Remove Comment Lines from a C++ Source Code File

In this project, you will write a C++ program that reads in a C++ source code file and removes any comment lines—that is, lines that begin with two forward slashes (//). This program does some of the work that is typically carried out by the C++ preprocessor, as you will learn in Chapter 8. After you delete the comment lines, save the file as Ch6-ip2.cpp in the Chapter6 folder on your Student Disk. You can use any C++ program in the Chapter6 folder as an input file.

Pointers

Introduction ▶ In this chapter you will review how to use the address operator, the indirection operator, and pointer variables in C++ programs. You will use pointers with arrays and strings to perform pointer arithmetic, which allows you to traverse arrays more efficiently than using indexes does. In addition, you will review passing arguments by address, arrays of pointers, and command line arguments.

Pointers

All variables are stored in memory at some address. A **pointer** is a variable that can store a memory address. You are already accustomed to using a variable name to directly access the value stored at the memory address associated with that variable. You use a pointer variable and the memory address stored in that pointer variable to indirectly access the value stored at a memory address.

Address Operator

The C++ **address operator** (&) is used to obtain the memory address that is associated with a variable. In Example 7-1, the program prints the value of the variable named x as well as the memory address associated with the variable named x.

Example 7-1

```
// Declares and initializes the variable named x.
int x = 5;
// The value 5 prints; this is the value
// stored at the memory address associated with x.
cout << x;
// The memory address associated with x will print.
cout << &x;
```

Declaring and Initializing a Pointer

You use the * symbol to declare a pointer variable. A data type must be explicitly associated with a pointer. Example 7-2 declares the variable named age as an integer and ptr_age as a pointer to an integer. It is important to declare age before ptr_age is initialized to ensure that the correct address will be stored in ptr_age. This C++ code initializes age to contain the integer value 21 and ptr_age to contain the address of age.

Example 7-2

```
int age = 21;
int* ptr_age = &age;
```

As Figure 7-1 shows, ptr_age now points to the integer stored in the memory address associated with age. The variable named age is stored at memory location 2000 and the variable named ptr_age is stored at memory location 2004. The contents of ptr_age is 2000, which is the address of age.

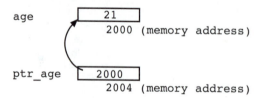

Figure 7-1: Pointer variable named ptr_age points to the contents of the variable named age

The Indirection Operator

The * symbol also serves as the **indirection operator**, which indirectly accesses the value to which a pointer points. This symbol is used in many ways in C++; C++ uses the context to determine the appropriate meaning. Example 7-3 shows uses of the * symbol to carry out multiplication, to declare a pointer variable, and to function as the indirection operator.

Example 7-3

```
int y = 5;
int x = y * 10;  // Multiplication
int* ptr_age = &x;  // Declaration of a pointer variable
cout << *ptr_age;  // Indirection operator; prints 50
```

Example 7-4 shows some additional examples in which the * symbol is used to declare a pointer variable and as the indirection operator.

Example 7-4

```
// Ex7-4.cpp
#include <iostream.h>

int main()
{
  int i = 777;
  int* ptr_i = &i;  // Assigns address of i to ptr.

  // Prints value of i.
  cout << "Value of i is: " << i << endl;
  // Prints what ptr_i points to.
  cout << "Value of i is: " << *ptr_i << endl;
  // Prints address of i.
  cout << "Address of i is: " << &i << endl;
  // Prints contents of ptr_i.
  cout << "Address of i is: " << ptr_i << endl;
  // Prints address of ptr_i.
  cout << "Address of ptr_i is: " << &ptr_i << endl;

  return 0;

}
```

The output of this program is as follows (memory addresses will vary):

```
Value of i is: 777
Value of i is: 777
Address of i is: 0x352E
Address of i is: 0x352E
Address of ptr_i is: 0x3530
```

The program shown in Example 7-5 declares pointer variables, assigns addresses to the pointer variables, and then uses the indirection operator to print the values to which the pointer variables point.

Example 7-5

```
// Ex7-5.cpp
#include <iostream.h>

int main()
{
  char c1, c2 = 'A';
  char* c1_ptr, *c2_ptr;

  c1_ptr = &c1;  // Assigns address of c1 to c1_ptr.
  c2_ptr = &c2;  // Assigns address of c2 to c2_ptr.
  // Makes c1_ptr point to the same value as c2_ptr.
  *c1_ptr = *c2_ptr;
  cout << "Value of c1 is " << c1 << endl;
  cout << "Value of c1 is " << *c1_ptr << endl;
  cout << "Value of c2 is " << c2 << endl;
  cout << "Value of c2 is " << *c2_ptr << endl;

  return 0;

}
```

Output:

```
Value of c1 is A
Value of c1 is A
Value of c2 is A
Value of c2 is A
```

Pointer Arithmetic

Pointer arithmetic allows you to add to pointers, subtract from pointers, compare pointers, and subtract one pointer from another. You must declare a pointer to point to the correct data type if pointer arithmetic is to work correctly.

When you add an integer to a pointer, the actual value added is the number of bytes or the size of the data type to which the pointer points. Example 7-6 illustrates the use of pointer arithmetic in a C++ code segment.

Example 7-6

```
char initial;
char* initial_ptr = &initial;
double price;
double* price_ptr = &price;

// Adds 8 (size of a double in bytes)
// to the value of price_ptr.
price_ptr++;
// Adds 1 (size of a char in bytes)
// to the value of initial_ptr.
initial_ptr++;
```

Pointer Arithmetic and Arrays

Pointer arithmetic is especially useful for sequentially accessing array elements. Using pointer arithmetic to sequentially access array elements is faster than using indexing, so you should use it as an alternative to array indexing.

Array names without an index are translated as the beginning or base memory address at which the array is stored. As shown in Example 7-7, if the base address of the array named ages is assigned to the variable named ptr_ages, then ptr_ages++ changes the address stored in ptr_ages to point to the next item in the ages array. By incrementing the pointer each time the loop executes, you can traverse the array via pointers.

Example 7-7

```cpp
// Ex7-7.cpp
#include <iostream.h>
const int SIZE = 6;

int main()
{
  int ages[SIZE] = {5, 10, 22, 81, 63, 25};
  int* ptr_ages;

  cout << "The ages in the array are: " << endl;

  // ptr_ages points to the beginning address
  // of the ages array.
  // Stay in this loop while the address stored in
  // ptr_ages is less than the address of ages[SIZE].
  // Increment the pointer each time the loop
  // is executed (pointer arithmetic).

  for(ptr_ages = ages; ptr_ages < &ages[SIZE]; ptr_ages++)
    cout << *ptr_ages << endl;

  return 0;
}
```

Output:

```
The ages in the array are:
5
10
22
81
63
25
```

You also could write the program shown in Example 7-7 using a while loop, as illustrated in Example 7-8.

Example 7-8

```
// Ex7-8.cpp
#include <iostream.h>
const int MAX_AGES = 6;
int main()
{
  int ages[MAX_AGES] = {5, 10, 22, 81, 63, 25};
  int* ptr_ages;

  cout << "The ages in the array are: " << endl;

  // ptr_ages points to the beginning address
  // of the ages array.
  ptr_ages = ages;

  // Stay in this loop while the address stored
  // in ptr_ages is less than the address of ages[MAX_AGES].
  while(ptr_ages < &ages[MAX_AGES])
  {
    cout << *ptr_ages << endl;
    // Increment the pointer each time the loop
    // is executed (pointer arithmetic).
    ptr_ages++;
  }

  return 0;

}
```

Output:

```
The ages in the array are:
5
10
22
81
63
25
```

Exercises

Exercise 7.1 ▶

Rewrite the home repair program you modified in Exercise 6-3 to use pointers and pointer arithmetic instead of array indexing. Review the problem description in Exercise 6-3 and then revise the program saved as Ch7-1.cpp in the Chapter7 folder on your Student Disk. Save your new program as Ch7-1a.cpp in the Chapter7 folder.

Exercise 7.2 ▶

The Super Sundries Company wants to use the program saved as Ch7-2.cpp in the Chapter7 folder on your Student Disk to help its sales representatives calculate their mileage reimbursement. The program prompts the salesperson to enter his or her mileage totals for each of the five days in a typical workweek, and then calculates the reimbursement total. Although the program compiles, it does not produce the correct output. Study the program and make the necessary changes. Save the corrected program as Ch7-2a.cpp in the Chapter7 folder.

Exercise 7.3 ▶

The Tele-Sales Corporation is a small telemarketing company that pays its telemarketers a monthly bonus based on their monthly sales totals (in dollars). Tele-Sales currently employs six telemarketers. Roberto Garcia, the owner, has asked you to write a C++ program that calculates the telemarketers' bonuses. Each telemarketer receives a 10 percent bonus on his or her total sales. A clerk enters monthly sales totals for each telemarketer. For last month, the program input consisted of $25,000.00, $75,000.00, $10,000.00, $25,000.00, $45,000.00, and $30,000.00. Your program should save the calculated monthly bonuses in an array. Display the output (Telemarketer Number, Monthly Sales Total, and Bonus) of this program as a formatted table. Use pointer arithmetic in your solution. Save your program as Ch7-3a.cpp in the Chapter7 folder on your Student Disk.

Strings and Pointer Arithmetic

You can employ pointer arithmetic to traverse a character array that contains a C++ string. Example 7-9 prints a first name and a last name stored in such a character array.

Example 7-9

```
// Ex7-9.cpp
#include <iostream.h>
const int MAX_NAME = 35;
int main()
{
  char name[MAX_NAME]= "Carmen Sanchez";
  char* ptr_name;
  char* first;
  char* last;

  // ptr_name points to the beginning of name array.
  ptr_name = name;
  // Loop until a space is reached.
  while(*ptr_name != ' ')
  // Increment ptr_name (pointer arithmetic).
    ptr_name++;
  *ptr_name = '\0';  // End of first string.
  first = name;
  cout << first << " ";
  last = ++ptr_name;  // Beginning of next string.
  cout << last << endl;

  return 0;

}
```

Output:

```
Carmen Sanchez
```

Exercises

Exercise 7.4 ▶

Modify the C++ program saved as Ch7-4.cpp in the Chapter7 folder on your Student Disk to use pointers and pointer arithmetic instead of arrays and indexing. Save the modified program as Ch7-4a.cpp in the Chapter7 folder.

Exercise 7.5 ▶

The C++ program saved as Ch7-5.cpp in the Chapter7 folder on your Student Disk copies one string to another, but currently produces the wrong output. Find and correct the errors, and then save the corrected program as Ch7-5a.cpp in the Chapter7 folder.

Exercise 7.6 ▶

Write a C++ program that finds a substring in a string. Your program should interactively ask the user for a string and a substring. Its output should announce whether the substring was found within the string. Save your program as Ch7-6a.cpp in the Chapter7 folder on your Student Disk. Test your program using the following data:

String	Substring
Encyclopedia	ped
Television	on
Bicycle	bike
Hello	eel
Goodbye	bye

Arrays of Pointers

Pointers can be stored in an array. By storing pointers to characters, the array can store the beginning memory address of a string. Example 7-10 declares the array named words as an array of pointers to characters that allows you to point to strings using the values stored in the array.

Example 7-10

```
// Ex7-10.cpp
#include <iostream.h>
const int MAX_WORDS = 15;
int main()
{
  char* words[MAX_WORDS];

  words[0] = "Hello";
  words[1] = "Bonjour";
  words[2] = "Goodbye";
  words[3] = "Au revoir";

  cout << words[0] << endl;
  cout << words[1] << endl;
  cout << words[2] << endl;
  cout << words[3] << endl;
  return 0;
}
```

Output:

```
Hello
Bonjour
Goodbye
Au revoir
```

As shown in Figure 7-2, the elements of the words array now contain the beginning memory addresses of the strings.

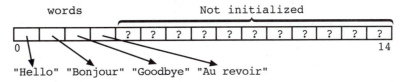

Figure 7-2: Array of character pointers that point to strings

Command Line Arguments

Two arguments may be passed to the main() function: argc and argv. The argc argument is an integer argument that represents the number of arguments on the command line. The value of argc is always at least 1 because the name of the program itself is an argument.

The argv argument is an array of character pointers—argv[0] points to the name of the program and argv[1] through argv[n] point to the strings included after the program name on the command line. For example, if you enter copy file1 file2 on the command line, then the value of argc is 3, the value of argv[0] is the beginning memory address of the string "copy", the value of argv[1] is the beginning memory address of the string "file 1", and the value of argv[2] is the beginning memory address of the string "file2". The C++ program in Example 7-11 uses argc and argv.

Example 7-11

```
// Ex7-11.cpp
#include <stdlib.h>
#include <iostream.h>

const int ARGNO = 3;
int main(int argc, char* argv[])
{
  int i;

  if(argc != ARGNO)
  {
    cout << "Usage:  ex7-11 file1 file2 " << endl;
    exit(1);
  }

  for(i = 0; i < argc; i++)
    cout << "ARGUMENT " << i << " is " << argv[i] << endl;
  return 0;

}
```

If the command line is ex7-11 file1 file2, then the output is as follows:

```
ARGUMENT 0 is ex7-11.exe
ARGUMENT 1 is file1
ARGUMENT 2 is file2
```

Exercises

Exercise 7.7 ▶

The C++ program saved as Ch7-7.cpp in the Chapter7 folder on your Student Disk counts the number of times that the word "the" appears in the file named cnt_the.dat. (The input file, cnt_the.dat, is stored in the Chapter7 folder as well.) Modify this program to receive the name of the file on the command line, allowing you to count the number of times the word "the" appears in any file. Save your modified program as Ch7-7a.cpp in the Chapter7 folder.

Exercise 7.8 ▶

The C++ program found in the file named Ch7-8.cpp in the Chapter7 folder on your Student Disk prints all command line arguments. If the program is invoked with the -u option as its first argument, all command line arguments are printed in uppercase letters. This program does not work correctly. Find and fix the errors, and then save the corrected program as Ch7-8a.cpp in the Chapter7 folder.

Exercise 7.9 ▶

Write a C++ program that finds the shortest word in a file. The name of the file should be included as a command line argument. Use any text file you like as the input file. Save your program as Ch7-9a.cpp in the Chapter7 folder on your Student Disk.

Passing Arguments by Address

Passing an argument by address allows the called function to change the value of the argument. It requires the use of pointers. As you know, a pointer is a variable that can store a memory address. The memory address of a local variable in the calling function is passed to the called function. The argument is declared as a pointer in the called function's definition and its declaration/prototype. You use the * symbol to declare a pointer argument. You also use the * symbol to dereference the pointer in the body of the function. The program shown in Example 7-12 uses pointers to pass arguments by address.

Example 7-12

```
// Ex7-12.cpp
#include <iostream.h>

// Function declaration; arguments declared as pointers.
void swap(int*, int*);

int main()
{
  int num1 = 5, num2 = 10;

  cout << "Value of num1 is " << num1 << ".\n";
  cout << "Value of num2 is " << num2 << ".\n";
  // Function call; pass the address of local variables.
  swap(&num1, &num2);
  cout << "Value of num1 is " << num1 << ".\n";
  cout << "Value of num2 is " << num2 << ".\n";

  return 0;
}
```

```
// Function definition; arguments declared as pointers.
void swap(int* val1, int* val2)
{
  int temp;
  // In function body, use the indirection operator
  // to dereference the variable.
  temp = *val1;
  *val1 = *val2;
  *val2 = temp;
}
```

The output of this program is as follows (notice that the values change):

```
Value of num1 is 5.
Value of num2 is 10.
Value of num1 is 10.
Value of num2 is 5.
```

Exercises

Exercise 7.10

The C++ program saved as Ch7-10.cpp in the Chapter7 folder on your Student Disk calls a function named `assign_random()`, which returns the random integer assigned. This random number is printed in the `main()` function. Modify this program to pass one integer argument to the `assign_random()` function by address. The function should assign a random number between 1 and 10 to the argument. In the `main()` function, print the random number assigned in the function. Save the modified program as Ch7-10a.cpp in the Chapter7 folder.

Exercise 7.11

The C++ program saved as Ch7-11.cpp in the Chapter7 folder on your Student Disk prints the area of a rectangle. Although the program compiles, it produces incorrect output. Find the errors and correct them. You should pass arguments by address. Save your corrected program as Ch7-11a.cpp in the Chapter7 folder.

Exercise 7.12

Write a C++ program that invokes an absolute value function. This `abs_val()` function should accept one argument (pass by address). If the value passed is negative, it should make the value positive. Print the value of the argument in the `main()` function two times—once before the function is called and again after the function is called. Save your program as Ch7-12a.cpp in the Chapter7 folder on your Student Disk.

S U M M A R Y

- A pointer is a variable that can store a memory address.

- You use the address operator (&) to obtain the memory address that is associated with a variable.

- You use the * symbol to declare a variable as a pointer. You always declare a pointer to point to a particular data type.

- You use the indirection operator (*) to indirectly access the value stored in a memory location to which a pointer points.

- You can sequentially access the data stored in arrays using pointer arithmetic. Pointer arithmetic is more efficient than using indexes when you need to access the elements of the array sequentially. Pointer arithmetic also works with strings.

- You can create arrays of pointers.

- To use command line arguments in a C++ program, you must use an array of character pointers named `argv[ ]`.

- You use pointers to pass an argument to a function by address. This form of argument passing allows the called function to change the actual value of an argument.

P R O G R E S S I V E   P R O J E C T S

1. Books and More

In Chapter 6, you added to the function that reads in the data from the inventory file. You also wrote functions that sort the inventory data by book title, list the complete inventory, list the inventory information for a single book, sell books, and save the inventory information to the inventory file, inBooks.dat, at the end of the day. In this assignment, you will write a function that allows you to accept a delivery of books. You will simulate taking a delivery by opening the file named newBooks.dat, saved in the Chapter7 folder on your Student Disk. The data in the newBooks.dat file have the same format as the data in the inventory file, inBooks.dat, except that no status data are available. All books delivered are assumed to be books that are in print. The function should read in the data for one book and then update the inventory data. If the book is already in your inventory, it should add to the quantity on hand. If the book is not in the inventory, the function should add it. Your inventory data are now in sorted order, so the function will have to sort the data again to ensure that the new book is placed in the correct order. The function should continue reading from the newBooks.dat file and update the inventory until it reaches EOF (end of file).

You also will write a function that prints a daily report. This report should include each book's title, ISBN number, and price; how many copies of the book were sold on that day; and the total sales amount for that book. The function should print this information in an attractively formatted table. After printing these data for each book, it should also print the total sales amount for all books sold on that day.

In future assignments, you will improve the methods for storing your data. Save your program as Ch7-pp1.cpp in the Chapter7 folder on your Student Disk.

2. Baseball Simulation

In Chapter 6, you added functionality to the baseball simulation project that lets you read in the rosters for both teams and then announce the two teams' rosters by printing the names of the players and their positions. In this assignment, you will add the ability to keep score by using two integer arrays and passing them to the appropriate functions. The arrays will store the number of runs scored by each team in each inning. This task might sound easy, but you must decide how to keep track of how many players are on base and when to add runs to the score. You can assume that runners advance one base for a single, two bases for a double, three bases for a triple, and four bases for a homerun. When runners advance far enough to score a run, they no longer need to advance beyond this point.

In future assignments, you will improve the methods for storing your data. Save your program as Ch7-pp2.cpp in the Chapter7 folder on your Student Disk.

 # INDEPENDENT PROJECTS

1. Better Browser Bookmark File

The Better Browser Software Company has hired you to help its team to develop a better Web browser. Your assignment is to maintain a user's bookmark file of URLs. Better Browser wants to increase the utility of a user's bookmark file by letting the user specify a category for each URL. The browser will then maintain the list of bookmarks sorted by category. Write a C++ program that reads in a user's bookmark file, which is stored in the file named bookmark.dat in the Chapter7 folder on your Student Disk. Each line in this file contains a URL and a general category. After the data are read from the input file, the program should sort the information by category and then display a menu that allows the user to add or delete a URL from the bookmark file. The bookmark file should remain in sorted order at all times. When the user wants to quit the program, you should save the updated bookmark file to the bookmark.dat file in the Chapter7 folder. Save your program as Ch7-ip1.cpp in the Chapter7 folder on your Student Disk.

2. BigBadBear Brokerage Account Manager

The BigBadBear Brokerage Company has asked you to write a stock account program. Each user will start with an account balance of $1,000. Your program should let the user choose the number of shares to purchase from a list of 10 stocks. Your program will read in the stock data from a file named stocks.dat that is saved in the Chapter7 folder on your Student Disk. This file includes the stock symbol, company name, and current price for the 10 stocks. After the user has purchased his or her stocks by entering the number of shares and the stock symbol, your program should simulate a day on the stock market. During the course of the day, the price of each stock will rise or fall by zero to 99 percent. At the end of the market day, your program should recalculate the value of the user's stock account and then provide the user with the option of buying more stock or selling stock that he or she already owns. After the user makes a decision, your program should simulate another day on the stock market. It should simulate a total of five days. After five days, your program should generate a final account report to display on the user's screen and to save in a file named account.dat in the Chapter7 folder on your Student Disk. Save your program as Ch7-ip2.cpp in the Chapter7 folder.

Structures
and Pointers

Introduction ▶ In this chapter you will use structures in C++ programming by creating structure templates, declaring structure variables, and referencing the members of structures. You also will learn how to work with arrays of structures, use pointers with structures, pass structures to functions, and return structures from functions. Finally, you will see how to nest and initialize structures.

Structure Definition

A **structure** is a group of data items that might have different data types, but that are given one name. A structure is a derived data type—the programmer creates it by using existing data types. Using structures in a C++ program allows you to organize data and treat a group of related data items as a single unit.

Structure Template

Syntax
· · · · · · · · · · · · · ·
▶ struct tag
{
   member declarations;
};

Because a structure is a derived data type, you must describe it using a **template**, which includes a **tag** (a name for the structure) and a list of the members of the structure. When creating a template, you must give a name and a data type to the members of the structure. Structure templates often are placed at the beginning of a file, so that the template will be available to all of the file's functions; you also can place structure templates in user-created header files. (You will learn about creating your own header files in Chapter 9.) When you #include a header file in a C++ program, the structure becomes available to every function in that file.

In Example 8-1, the structure template describes an employee structure with four members. Three of the members are character arrays that store the employee's Social Security number, last name, and first name; the fourth member is a double that stores the employee's salary.

Example 8-1

```
const int LENGTH = 20;
struct employee
{
   char ssn[LENGTH];
   char lname[LENGTH];
   char fname[LENGTH];
   double salary;
};
```

Structure Declaration

After creating a structure template, you can declare variables of that derived data type. The code shown in Example 8-2 uses the employee structure template to declare the variables manager and programmers and, at the same time, reserves memory for these variables.

Example 8-2

```
// Declares and reserves memory for one employee
// structure.
employee manager;
// Declares and reserves contiguous memory
// for 45 employee structures.
employee programmers[45];
```

Exercise

Exercise 8.1 ▶ Mr. Food, a local restaurant critic, would like to store the following information for each restaurant that he reviews: name, address, city, telephone number, food type (such as Italian, Mexican, Chinese, American, and so on), most expensive menu item, least expensive menu item, and a rating (one to four spoons, where four spoons is the highest rating). On a piece of paper, create a structure template for this information and then declare a variable named `rest1` of this structure type.

Syntax

▶ structure_name.member_name

Referencing Structure Members

You use the **dot operator** (.), which sometimes is called the **member operator**, to reference the individual members of a structure. Structure members can be used in your C++ programs in the same way that you would use variables. For example, if the structure member is a string, then you could use the `strlen()` function to find its length. If the structure member is an integer, you could multiply it by 10 or divide it by 2.

Example 8-3 uses a structure's members in a C++ program.

Example 8-3

```cpp
// Ex8-3.cpp
const int LENGTH = 20;
// Template for an employee structure.
struct employee
{
  char ssn[LENGTH];
  char lname[LENGTH];
  char fname[LENGTH];
  double salary;
};

#include <iostream.h>

int main()
{
  // Declaration, reserves memory for an
  // employee structure.
  employee manager;

  // Gets user's first and last names.
  cout << "Please enter your last name: ";
  cin.getline(manager.lname,LENGTH);
  cout << "Please enter your first name: ";
  cin.getline(manager.fname,LENGTH);

  // Gets user's Social Security number.
  cout << "Please enter your Social Security number: ";
  cin.getline(manager.ssn,LENGTH);
```

```
// Gets user's salary.
cout << "Please enter your salary: ";
cin >> manager.salary;

// Calculates manager's pay increase.
manager.salary *= 1.20;

// Prints name, new salary, and Social
// Security number.
cout << "Name:   " << manager.fname << " " \
  << manager.lname << endl;
cout << "Salary:  " << manager.salary << endl;
cout << "SSN:  " << manager.ssn << endl;

return 0;

}
```

If you enter the following information into this program,

```
Smith
Raymond
888-88-8888
125000
```

then the program output is as follows:

```
Name:  Raymond Smith
Salary:  150000
SSN:  888-88-8888
```

Exercises

Exercise 8.2 ▶

The C++ program saved as Ch8-2.cpp in the Chapter8 folder on your Student Disk reads a month, day, and year and then prints it in mm/dd/year format. Modify this program so that it uses a structure to store the date information. Save your modified program as Ch8-2a.cpp in the Chapter8 folder.

Exercise 8.3 ▶

The sponsors of the Crosstown Marathon have asked you to write a C++ program that prompts a runner to enter his or her name and race finish time in hours, minutes, and seconds. You are using a structure to store the hours, minutes, and seconds of this time, and another variable to store the name. Your program, which is saved as Ch8-3.cpp in the Chapter8 folder on your Student Disk, prints the information stored in the structure after reading it, but it does not compile. Find and fix the errors, and then save the corrected program as Ch8-3a.cpp in the Chapter8 folder.

Exercise 8.4 ▶

Write a C++ program that uses a structure to store a date (month, day, year). Your program should ask the user to enter a date and then print the next day's date. For example, if the user enters 2/27/00, then your program should print 2/28/00; 3/31/00 should become 4/1/00; 12/31/00 should become 1/1/01; and so on. Your program should ignore leap years. Save your program as Ch8-4a.cpp in the Chapter8 folder on your Student Disk.

Arrays of Structures

You use an array of structures just as you would use any other array. Example 8-4 shows a C++ program that uses an array of structures.

Example 8-4

```cpp
// Ex8-4.cpp
const int LENGTH = 20;
// employee structure template.
struct employee
{
  int id;
  char lname[LENGTH];
  char fname[LENGTH];
  double salary;
};

#include <iostream.h>

int main()
{
  const int MAX_PROG = 5;
  // Array of 5 employee structures.
  employee programmers[MAX_PROG];

  int i;
  // Gets last and first names of 5 programmers.
  for(i = 0; i < MAX_PROG; i++)
  {
    cout << "Please enter your last name: ";
    cin.getline(programmers[i].lname,LENGTH);
    cout << "Please enter your first name: ";
    cin.getline(programmers[i].fname,LENGTH);
  }

  for(i = 0; i < MAX_PROG; i++)
  {
    // Assigns an ID number.
    programmers[i].id = i + 1;
    // Assigns a salary.
    programmer[i].salary = 35000.00;
    // Calculates a new salary.
    programmer[i].salary *= (i + 1);
  }

  // Prints ID number, name, and salary for 5 programmers.
  for(i = 0; i < MAX_PROG; i++)
  {
    cout << "Employee ID Number: " \
      << programmers[i].id << endl;
    cout << "Employee Name      : " \
      << programmers[i].fname << " " \
      << programmers[i].lname << endl;
```

```
        cout << "Salary                :" << \
          programmers[i].salary << endl;
    }

    return 0;

}
```

If the input to this program is

```
Smith JoAnn
Smith Raymond
Moriarty Timothy
Johnson Jeanne
Johnson John
```

then the output is as follows:

```
Employee ID Number: 1
Employee Name       : JoAnn Smith
Salary              : 35000
Employee ID Number: 2
Employee Name       : Raymond Smith
Salary              : 70000
Employee ID Number: 3
Employee Name       : Timothy Moriarty
Salary              : 105000
Employee ID Number: 4
Employee Name       : Jeanne Johnson
Salary              : 140000
Employee ID Number: 5
Employee Name       : John Johnson
Salary              : 175000
```

Exercises

Exercise 8.5 ▶

MODIFY

The C++ program saved as Ch8-5.cpp in the Chapter8 folder on your Student Disk uses parallel arrays to convert a date to a Julian date (1–365). Modify this program so that it uses an array of structures instead of parallel arrays. Save the modified program as Ch8-5a.cpp in the Chapter8 folder.

Exercise 8.6 ▶

DEBUG

The C++ program saved as Ch8-6.cpp in the Chapter8 folder on your Student Disk stores address book information in parallel arrays. When you enter a name, the program prints the name, address, city, state, telephone number, and e-mail address for that person. You modified this program to use an array of structures instead of the parallel arrays, but now it does not work correctly. Find and fix the errors, and then save the corrected program as Ch8-6a.cpp in the Chapter8 folder.

Exercise 8.7 ▶

DEVELOP

Charlene Ramirez, the owner of the Value Video Store, has asked you to write a C++ program that allows her to enter a video's unique ID number, and then responds with the number of copies of the video with that ID number currently in her inventory. The inventory is stored in a file named video.dat in the Chapter8 folder on your Student Disk. Data are stored in this file in a format in which the video ID number appears on one line and the number of copies appears on the next line. The inventory can hold a maximum of 100 videos. Use an array of structures to store the inventory. Save the program as Ch8-7a.cpp in the Chapter8 folder.

Pointers and Structures

Pointers can be used to point to structures. In Example 8-5, the code declares a pointer to a structure and assigns the memory address of the manager structure to the pointer named `ptr_mgr`.

Example 8-5

```
employee manager;
employee* ptr_mgr;
ptr_mgr = &manager;
```

When you use a pointer to access the members of a structure indirectly, you use the **pointer member operator** (`->`), which is written as a dash and a greater than symbol, with no space separating the two symbols. Example 8-6 shows uses of the dot and pointer member operators in a C++ program.

Example 8-6

```cpp
// Ex8-6.cpp
const int LENGTH = 40;
#include <iostream.h>

// Template for a person structure.
struct person
{
  char name[LENGTH];
  int id;
  double salary;
};

// Function declaration.
// Expects two arguments, an array of person structures,
// and an integer.
void get_data(person[], int);

int main()
{
  const int MAX_PROGRAMMERS = 5;
  // Array of 5 person structures.
  person programmers[MAX_PROGRAMMERS];
  int i;

  // Passes an array of person structures and
  // an integer to get_data.
  get_data(programmers, MAX_PROGRAMMERS);
  // Prints name, ID number, and salary of 5 programmers.
  for(i = 0; i < MAX_PROGRAMMERS; i++)
  {
    cout << "NAME    :" << programmers[i].name << endl;
    cout << "ID #    :" << programmers[i].id << endl;
    cout << "SALARY  :" << programmers[i].salary << endl;
  }
  return 0;
}
```

```
// Function declaration.
// This function returns nothing and expects two arguments:
// an array of person structures named people and an integer
// named size. This function gets a name, Social
// Security number, and salary from the user and then
// calculates a new salary based on the existing salary.

void get_data(person people[], int size)
{
  // Pointer used to traverse array of person structures.
  person* ptr;
  // Points to beginning of array;
  // stays in loop until pointer is incremented beyond
  // end of array; increments pointer each time through
  // loop (pointer arithmetic).
  for(ptr = people; ptr < &people[size]; ptr++)
  {
    // Gets name and salary from user.
    cout << "Enter your name: ";
    cin >> ptr->name;
    cout << "Enter your salary: ";
    cin >> ptr->salary;
    // Calculates new salary.
    if(ptr->salary < 50000.00)
      ptr->salary *= 1.10;
    else
      ptr->salary *= 1.15;
    // Gets ID number from user.
    cout << "Enter your ID number: ";
    cin >> ptr->id;
  }
  return;
}
```

If the input to this program is:

```
JoAnn
23000.00
123
Ray
45000.00
234
Timothy
67000.00
678
Ricardo
35500.00
256
Paulo
89000.00
890
```

then the output is as follows:

```
NAME     :JoAnn
ID #     :123
SALARY   :25300
NAME     :Ray
ID #     :234
SALARY   :49500
NAME     :Timothy
ID #     :678
SALARY   :77050
NAME     :Ricardo
ID #     :256
SALARY   :39050
NAME     :Paulo
ID #     :890
SALARY   :102350
```

Exercises

Exercise 8.8 ▶

In Exercise 8-5, you modified a C++ program to use an array of structures. A version of this program is saved as Ch8-8.cpp in the Chapter8 folder on your Student Disk. Modify this program to use a pointer to access the array of structures. Save your modified program as Ch8-8a.cpp in the Chapter8 folder.

Exercise 8.9 ▶

In Exercise 8-6, you debugged an address book program. Now, you have modified this program to use a pointer to access the members of structures. The modified program, which is saved as Ch8-9.cpp in the Chapter8 folder on your Student Disk, does not compile. Find and fix the errors so that the program will run correctly, and then save the corrected program as Ch8-9a.cpp in the Chapter8 folder.

Exercise 8.10 ▶

Rewrite the program you wrote in Exercise 6-9 so that it uses an array of structures instead of parallel arrays. The revised program should use a pointer to traverse the array of structures rather than an index. The program should keep track of the number of calories and the number of fat grams contained in each of 10 food products. The food products have been assigned the numbers 0 through 9 to preserve their anonymity. The relevant data are found in the file named food.dat in the Chapter8 folder on your Student Disk. This information appears in the following format: number of calories on one line, and the number of fat grams on the next line. For example, the calories on the first line are for product number 0 and the fat grams on the next line are for product number 0. Read the data into an array of structures and then print the product number with the fewest calories and the product number with the fewest fat grams. Save your program as Ch8-10a.cpp in the Chapter8 folder.

Passing Structures to Functions

You can pass structures to a function, and a function can return a structure. In Example 8-7, the C++ program passes a structure to a function named `increase_pay()` and returns a structure from the same function.

Example 8-7

```cpp
// Ex8-7.cpp
const int NAME_LEN = 40;
const int INIT_LEN = 10;
#include <iostream.h>

//  person structure template.
struct person
{
  char name[NAME_LEN];
  char initials[INIT_LEN];
  double salary;
};

// Function declarations.
void get_data(person[], int);
int check_sal(person*);
person increase_pay(person);

int main()
{
  const int MAX_PROGRAMMERS = 5;
  // Array of 5 person structures.
  person programmers[MAX_PROGRAMMERS];
  int i;

  // Passes an array of structures and
  // an integer to get_data.
  get_data(programmers, MAX_PROGRAMMERS);

  for(i = 0; i < MAX_PROGRAMMERS; i++)
  {
    // Passes a structure and returns a structure.
    programmers[i] = increase_pay(programmers[i]);
    // Passes a pointer to a structure.
    if(check_sal(&programmers[i]))
    {
      cout << "NAME    :" << programmers[i].name << endl;
      cout << "INITIALS:" << programmers[i].initials << endl;
      cout << "SALARY  :" << programmers[i].salary << endl;
    }
  }

  return 0;
}

// This function expects a pointer to a person structure
// and returns true (1) if the salary member
// of the structure pointed to by this_emp is greater
// than 1000 or false (0) if it is less than/equal to 1000.

int check_sal(person* this_emp)
{
  return this_emp->salary > 1000;
}
```

```
// This function expects a person structure that will
// be referred to as this_emp in the function. It
// calculates a 10% increase and stores the new salary in
// this_emp's salary member. The function returns the modified
// person structure.

person increase_pay(person this_emp)
{
  this_emp.salary *= 1.10;
  return this_emp;
}


// This function returns nothing and expects two arguments:
// an array of person structures named people and an integer
// named size. This function gets a name, Social Security
// number, and salary from the user and stores the
// values in the array of structures.

void get_data(person people[], int size)
{
  person* ptr;
  for(ptr = people; ptr < &people[size]; ptr++)
  {
    cout << "Enter your name: ";
    cin >> ptr->name;
    cout << "Enter your salary: ";
    cin >> ptr->salary;
    cout << "Enter your initials: ";
    cin >> ptr->initials;
  }
  return;
}
```

If the input to this program is:

```
JoAnn
1500.00
jas
Raymond
300.00
rds
Timothy
4500.00
tjm
John
250.00
jej
Jeanne
5000.00
jij
```

then the output is as follows:

```
NAME        :JoAnn
Initials    :jas
SALARY      :1650
NAME        :Timothy
Initials    :tjm
SALARY      :4950
NAME        :Jeanne
Initials    :jij
SALARY      :5500
```

Exercises

Exercise 8.11 ▶

The C++ program saved as Ch8-11.cpp in the Chapter8 folder on your Student Disk reads in the name, salary, and years of service for an employee of the XYZ Candy Store from a file named candy.dat. It uses parallel arrays to store the data and passes an array to a function to calculate employees' raises. Modify this program so that it uses an array of structures to store the data. Save your modified program as Ch8-11a.cpp in the Chapter8 folder.

Exercise 8.12 ▶

The college basketball coach has asked you to write a C++ program that reads in player statistics, sorts the data based on the player's name, and prints a report. Your program does not compile, however. Find and fix the errors in the program stored in the file named Ch8-12.cpp in the Chapter8 folder on your Student Disk, and then save the corrected program as Ch8-12a.cpp. The player statistics are stored in a file named stats.dat in the Chapter8 folder.

Exercise 8.13 ▶

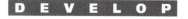

Rewrite the Goodebody Health Food Store program (from Exercise 6-24) using structures instead of parallel arrays. In Exercise 6-24, you wrote a function that reads in the names of products and their prices from a file named health.dat. The input file, health.dat, is stored in the Chapter8 folder on your Student Disk. In your original program, you stored the names in one array and the prices in another. Now, you will use an array of structures. The maximum number of products remains 50. The earlier program included another function that printed the names of the products and their prices. Your new program also should print the names and prices of products. Save your new program as Ch8-13a.cpp in the Chapter8 folder on your Student Disk.

Nested Structures

In C++, you can nest a structure within another structure. Example 8-8 shows a template for a nested structure and the variable declaration. It also illustrates how the nested structure is processed.

Example 8-8

```
// Ex8-8.cpp
#include <iostream.h>
#include <string.h>

const int NAME_LEN = 40;
const int ID_LEN = 10;
```

```
// date structure template.
struct date
{
  int month;
  int day;
  int year;
};

// customer_info structure template.
struct customer_info
{
  char customer_id[ID_LEN];
  char acct_type;
  char name[NAME_LEN];
  double balance;
  date pay_date;  // Nested structure
};

int main()
{
  // Variable of type customer_info structure named customer.
  customer_info customer;

  // Assigns values to members of the structure.
  strcpy(customer.customer_id, "A456X");
  strcpy(customer.name, "Mary Sanchez");
  customer.acct_type = 'N'; // N is for New.
  customer.balance = 2300.50;

  // Assigns values to members of the nested structure.
  customer.pay_date.month = 12;
  customer.pay_date.day = 15;
  customer.pay_date.year = 2000;

  cout << "Customer ID :" << customer.customer_id << endl;
  cout << "Name        :" << customer.name << endl;
  cout << "Acct Type   :" << customer.acct_type << endl;
  cout << "Balance     :" << customer.balance << endl;
  cout << "Payment Date:" << customer.pay_date.month << \
    "-" << customer.pay_date.day << \
    "-" << customer.pay_date.year << endl;
  return 0;
}
```

The output of this program is:

```
Acct No.    :A456X
Name        :Mary Sanchez
Acct Type   :N
Balance     :2300.5
Payment Date:12-15-2000
```

Exercises

Exercise 8.14 ▶

The C++ program saved as Ch8-14.cpp in the Chapter8 folder on your Student Disk maintains a customer mailing list for the owner of the Big Bauble Jewelry Store. It reads mailing list data from a data file named jewelry.dat saved in the Chapter8 folder and then prints a mailing list. The program currently uses two parallel arrays of structures to store the customer information. The `customer` structure includes the following members: `name`, `phone`, and `e_mail`. The `address` structure includes the following members: `street`, `city`, `state`, and `zip`. You would like to modify this program so that it uses a nested structure. The members of the new structure will be `name`, `addr_info`, `phone`, and `e_mail`. The member `addr_info` should be an `address` structure that is nested in a `customer` structure. Make the necessary changes and save the modified program as Ch8-14a.cpp in the Chapter8 folder.

Exercise 8.15 ▶

You have written a C++ program to use as an appointment book. Your goal is to enter a customer's name, business affiliation, and telephone number as well as the scheduled date and time of your appointment with that customer. Your program, which is stored in a file named Ch8-15.cpp in the Chapter8 folder on your Student Disk, does not work correctly. Find and fix the errors, and then save your corrected program as Ch8-15a.cpp.

Exercise 8.16 ▶

Write a C++ program that stores information about players who have been selected as participants in a Fantasy Football League. The data for this program are saved in a file named fantasy.dat in the Chapter8 folder on your Student Disk. This file contains the following information about each player: name, NFL team, position, and Fantasy League owner's name. Your program should read these data into an array of nested structures and then create an attractively formatted report listing the information. Save your program as Ch8-16a.cpp in the Chapter8 folder.

Initializing Structures

You can initialize a structure when you declare it by listing the individual values that correspond to the data members of the structure in curly braces and separating them with commas. In Example 8-9, the code initializes a `customer_info` structure.

Example 8-9

```
const int NAME_LEN = 40;
const int ID_LEN = 10;
// date structure template.
struct date
{
  int month;
  int day;
  int year;
};
```

```
// customer_info structure template.
struct customer_info
{
  char customer_id[ID_LEN];
  char acct_type;
  char name[NAME_LEN];
  double balance;
  date pay_date;
};

// Declares and initializes an account structure
// named customer.
customer_info customer =
    {"A567X", 'E', "John Singh", 586.50, 5, 15, 2000};
```

In Example 8-10, the code initializes an array of date structures.

Example 8-10

```
const int MAX_BDAYS = 5;
const int NAME_LEN = 20;
// date structure template.
struct date
{
  char name[NAME_LEN];
  int month;
  int day;
  int year;
};

// Declares and initializes an array of 5 date structures.
// The array is named birthdays.
date birthdays[MAX_BDAYS] = {   {"Allen", 6,14,1957},
                                {"Wu",    7,24,1997},
                                {"Helga", 1,1,1990},
                                {"Tejas", 5,7,1956},
                                {"Hardi", 3,14,1945} } ;
```

Exercises

Exercise 8.17 ▶

Review the program specification found in Exercise 8-5. Use the file named Ch8-17.cpp in the Chapter8 folder on your Student Disk to make the same modification you made in Exercise 8-5. This time, however, you should use an initialization statement to populate the array of structures. Save the modified program as Ch8-17a.cpp in the Chapter8 folder.

Exercise 8.18 ▶

D E B U G

Ms. Friend, your daughter's third-grade teacher, has asked you to write a C++ program to store her students' names and telephone numbers. The student data are saved in a file named student.dat in the Chapter8 folder on your Student Disk. You want to use an initialization statement to populate an array of structures with these data. Your program, which is saved as Ch8-18.cpp in the Chapter8 folder, does not compile, so you do not know whether it produces the correct output. Find and fix the errors, and then save the corrected program as Ch8-18a.cpp in the Chapter8 folder.

Exercise 8.19 ▶

Rewrite the C++ program you developed in Exercise 6-30 to use an array of structures instead of parallel arrays. The program should allow you to read an English-French dictionary into an array of structures. The structures should hold an English word and its French equivalent. The dictionary data are stored in a file named dict.dat in the Chapter8 folder on your Student Disk. Sort the array of structures by the English word. Your revised program should then allow a user to look up an English word and print the French equivalent. Your dictionary should be able to store a maximum of 50 English and French words. Save the new program as Ch8-19a.cpp in the Chapter8 folder on your Student Disk.

S U M M A R Y

■ A structure is a group of data items that might have different data types but that are given one name.

■ You can organize data in your C++ programs using structures.

■ Before declaring variables of a particular structure type, you must provide a structure template.

■ You must declare a structure before using it in a C++ program.

■ The dot operator (.) is used to reference the members of a structure.

■ You can create an array of structures in C++.

■ You can use a pointer variable to contain the address of a structure.

■ The pointer member operator (->) is used to reference the members of a structure that you are using a pointer variable to point to.

■ In C++, you can pass a structure to a function and return a structure from a function.

■ You can nest structures within other structures.

■ To initialize a structure, list the individual member values within curly braces and separate them with commas.

P R O G R E S S I V E   P R O J E C T S

1. Books and More

In Chapter 7, you added the functionality to take a delivery of books and update your inventory by adding to the quantity on hand or adding the information about a book to the inventory. You also developed the functionality to print a daily report. Congratulations are in order—you now have a working version of this project.

In this assignment, you will improve the method for storing the inventory data by modifying your program so that it uses an array of structures. Save your project as Ch8-pp1.cpp in the Chapter8 folder on your Student Disk. In Chapter 9, you will use preprocessor directives to organize your project.

2. Baseball Simulation

In Chapter 7, you added the ability to keep score in your baseball game. Congratulations are in order—you now have a working version of this project.

In this assignment, you will modify the method for storing the names and positions of the players by using an array of structures instead of parallel arrays. Save your project as Ch8-pp2.cpp in the Chapter8 folder on your Student Disk.

INDEPENDENT PROJECTS

1. Run-time Error Messages

In this project, you will simulate incurring run-time errors and printing a descriptive error message for the user. For example, error number 5 is a data type mismatch. When error 5 occurs, your program should print something like the following message:

```
Error Number:  5
Description:  Data Type Mismatch
```

You should use an array of structures to store the information about errors. The error numbers and their descriptions are saved in a file named errors.dat in the Chapter8 folder on your Student Disk. Use the random number generator to raise errors. For example, when the random number generator returns a 5, your program should report error number 5. Save your project as Ch8-ip1.cpp in the Chapter8 folder on your Student Disk.

2. Personal Computer Comparative Analysis

Write a C++ program that reads in the following data about 10 PCs: vendor name, model, price, RAM (in megabytes), hard disk size (in gigabytes), monitor (y or n), and monitor size. The data are stored in a file named pc_info.dat in the Chapter8 folder on your Student Disk.

After storing the data in an array of structures, your program should prompt the user to look up data about the PCs. For example, the user should be able to find specific information about every PC, all of the information about every PC, all of the information about one PC, or specific information about one PC. Provide a menu similar to the following from which your user can make choices:

```
Enter  1) list all information about one PC
       2) list all information about all PCs
       3) list some information about one PC
       4) list some information about all PCs
       5) I am finished looking up information about PCs
```

Your program should prompt the user for additional information depending on which choice is selected. For example, if the user chooses 3 from the menu, your program should prompt the user for the name of the PC and which features to consider. Save your program as Ch8-ip2.cpp in the Chapter8 folder on your Student Disk.

The Preprocessor

Introduction ▶ In this chapter, you will learn about and use the C++ preprocessor directives #define, which creates symbolic constants and macros, and #include, which includes system-supplied and user-created header files. You also will review the preprocessor statements used for conditional compilation.

Definition

The **C++ preprocessor** is a program that processes your C++ source code before the compiler processes it. Any line in your source code file that begins with a pound sign (#) is called a **preprocessor directive**. Although you can place preprocessor directives anywhere in a file, they are usually inserted at the beginning of the source code file or placed in header files. You place the pound sign in the first column. Preprocessor directives are not C++ statements, so they do not end with a semicolon. These directives instruct the preprocessor to make changes to your C++ source code, such as defining constants and macros, including files, and performing conditional compilation.

Symbolic Constants

Syntax

▶ #define SYMBOL token

When you use symbolic constants in a C++ program, the preprocessor will find all references to the SYMBOL in your source code and replace it with the token that you supplied in the `#define` statement. C++ programming convention is to use upper-case letters for the SYMBOL. Notice that the `#define` preprocessor directive does not end with a semicolon, and you do not place an equals sign between the SYMBOL and the token. SYMBOLs, like variables, should be given meaningful names.

Example 9-1 shows the code to create a symbolic constant named `PI`. Each time the preprocessor encounters the SYMBOL `PI` in the C++ source code, the preprocessor will replace `PI` with the value 3.14159. The preprocessor, however, will not change the characters "PI" within a string constant.

Example 9-1

```
#define PI 3.14159
double area_circle;
double radius = 7.0;

area_circle = PI * (radius * radius);
cout << "The value of PI is " << PI << endl;
```

Symbolic constants are used extensively in C programming. C++ offers an alternative to `#define`. As you have already learned, placing the keyword `const` before a variable allows you to create a constant. The use of `#define` differs from the use of `const` as follows:

- `#define` does not allocate storage as `const` does.
- `#define` remains visible from its location in the file to the end of the file; `const`, on the other hand, follows the rules of variable storage classes.

Using a symbolic constant in a file other than the file in which it is defined results in a syntax error.

Exercises

Exercise 9.1 ▶

The C++ program saved as Ch9-1.cpp in the Chapter9 folder on your Student Disk does not use symbolic constants. Review this program and then rewrite it using symbolic constants where appropriate. Save your modified program as Ch9-1a.cpp in the Chapter9 folder.

Exercise 9.2 ▶

The C++ program saved as Ch9-2.cpp in the Chapter9 folder on your Student Disk prompts the user to enter a number of hours, minutes, and seconds, and then converts the total time to seconds. The program does not compile, however, so you do not know whether it produces the correct output. Find and fix the errors, and then save the corrected program as Ch9-2a.cpp in the Chapter9 folder.

Exercise 9.3 ▶

D E V E L O P

Write a C++ program that defines a list of error messages using #define preprocessor statements. If an error occurs in your program, you can use the symbolic constant to print an appropriate error message. In this program, you will create the symbolic constants and then print them. For example,

```
#define PRINTER "Printer not responding."
cout << PRINTER;
```

The following error messages are possible:

Printer not responding.

Age entered must be greater than 21.

Social Security number must have nine digits.

Save your program as Ch9-3a.cpp in the Chapter9 folder.

Macros

Syntax

▶ #define SYMBOL([arg, arg]) token

A **macro** is a small set of statements that can accept arguments. You create a macro using a #define statement. By convention, macros, like symbolic constants, are named with all uppercase letters and should be given meaningful names. No space should separate the SYMBOL and the opening parenthesis—including any space will result in a compiler error. An expression should be fully parenthesized when operators are used in the token.

The program in Example 9-2 creates the SQUARE macro and uses it in the program.

Example 9-2

```
// Ex9-2.cpp
#include <iostream.h>
#define SQUARE(x) ((x) * (x)) // Full set of parentheses.

int main()
{
  int num1, num2;

  num1 = SQUARE(3); // Becomes ((3) * (3))
  num2 = SQUARE(num1 + 1);  // Becomes ((num1+1) * (num1+1))
  cout << "Value of num1 is: " << num1 << endl;
  cout << "Value of num2 is: " << num2 << endl;

  return 0;
}
```

The output of this program is as follows:

```
Value of num1 is: 9
Value of num2 is: 100
```

When the preprocessor finishes processing your source code, your source code changes to the following:

```
SQUARE(x)((x) * (x))
num1 = ((3) * (3));
num2 = ((num1 + 1) * (num1 + 1));
    // Notice the importance of the parentheses in the macro.
```

To continue a macro on more than one line, type a backslash (\) at the end of the previous line.

Macros and functions are similar in that both can receive arguments and are written to accomplish a specific task. Macros and functions do have differences, however. A macro will execute more rapidly than a function because the code is replaced in-line, whereas calling a function creates system overhead because program control must be transferred to the called function and then returned to the calling function.

If you use a macro several times in a program, the size of the executable program will increase because the macro's code will be repeated in several locations in the program.

Other differences between macros and functions are as follows:

- Macros cannot return values.
- Macros cannot be written recursively.
- Macros are often harder to debug than functions.

Macros are used extensively in C programming. In C++, you can write in-line functions to reduce the need to use macros. (A full discussion of in-line functions is beyond the scope of this book.)

Exercises

Exercise 9.4 ▶

MODIFY

Professor Hacker wrote the C++ program saved as Ch9-4.cpp in the Chapter9 folder on your Student Disk to help her students understand pointers. She has asked you to rewrite it to demonstrate the use of macros in a C++ program. Write a macro that prints the six values that are currently printed by the cout statements. Replace each cout statement with the macro. Save the modified program as Ch9-4a.cpp in the Chapter9 folder.

Exercise 9.5 ▶

DEBUG

The C++ program saved as Ch9-5.cpp in the Chapter9 folder on your Student Disk uses a macro to swap two integer values. The program does not compile, however, so you are not sure whether it produces correct output. Find and fix the errors, and then save the corrected program as Ch9-5a.cpp in the Chapter9 folder.

Exercise 9.6 ▶

DEVELOP

Write a C++ program that uses a MAX macro to determine which of two integers has a greater value. The macro should accept the two integers as arguments. Store the larger value in a variable named bigger, and then print the value of bigger. Save your program as Ch9-6a.cpp in the Chapter9 folder on your Student Disk.

▶ // C++ header file.
#include <filename.h>
// User header file.
#include "filename.h"

Header Files

Using the #include preprocessor directive causes a copy of a file, called a header file, to be included in your C++ program at the point at which the preprocessor encounters this directive. Header files usually contain #define statements, function prototypes, external variable declarations, and structure templates.

By convention, header files are named using a .h extension. In addition, #include statements generally appear at the beginning of a C++ source code file or in another .h file.

The C++ compiler supplies several header files. To include these header files in your programs, place the filename within angle brackets in the #include statement (for example, #include <iostream.h>).

You also can create your own header files. To include user-created header files, place the filename within double quotation marks in the #include statement. The preprocessor will look for this file in your current directory. You can use full and relative pathnames when including your own header files if they are not stored in the current directory. Example 9-3 illustrates the use of #include preprocessor directives.

Example 9-3

```
#include <iostream.h>
#include "myhead.h"
#include "/usr/jsmith/myhead.h"    // UNIX
#include "C:\\myhead.h"            // Windows
```

Exercises

Exercise 9.7 ▶

In Exercise 8-2, you modified a C++ program so that it used a structure to store a year, month, and day instead of storing the data in three separate variables. In this exercise, you will make the same modification, but you will store the structure template in a separate header file and #include the header file in your program. The program to be modified is saved as Ch9-7.cpp in the Chapter9 folder on your Student Disk. Save the revised program as Ch9-7a.cpp in the Chapter9 folder.

Exercise 9.8 ▶

The C++ program saved as Ch9-8.cpp in the Chapter9 folder on your Student Disk is a password verification program that asks a user to enter a password and then checks whether this password is valid. If the password is invalid, then the program terminates. If the password is valid, then the program welcomes the user to the system. This program is not compiling, however, so you cannot test it to see whether it runs correctly. Find and fix the errors, and then save the corrected program as Ch9-8a.cpp in the Chapter9 folder.

Exercise 9.9 ▶

D E V E L O P

Write a C++ program that manages data about 10 college students. Store the following data for each student: name (first and last), major, and number of credits earned. Your program should open the file named majors.dat (which is saved in the Chapter9 folder on your Student Disk), read the data stored in this file into an array of structures, and then print a report that lists each student's name and status. The status is defined as freshman, sophomore, junior, or senior. A freshman has 0 to 33 credits, a sophomore has 34 to 66 credits, a junior has 67 to 99 credits, and a senior has 100 to 132 credits. Save the structure template for a student in a header file named student.h and #include this file in your program. Save your program as Ch9-9a.cpp in the Chapter9 folder on your Student Disk.

Conditional Compilation

C++ preprocessor directives allow you to write programs that will conditionally add lines to your programs, thereby enabling you to create several versions of a single program. Figure 9-1 lists the conditional compilation preprocessor directives.

Directive	Description
`#if`	Include the lines in the file if an expression is true.
`#ifdef`	Include the lines in the file if a symbolic constant is defined.
`#ifndef`	Include the lines in the file if a symbolic constant is not defined.
`#undef`	Undefine a symbolic constant before the symbolic constant's value may be changed with another `#define`.
`#endif`	Mark the end of an `#if`, `#ifdef`, or `#ifndef` statement.

Figure 9-1: Conditional compilation preprocessor directives

Including a header file more than once in a C++ program results in a compile-time error. You can use conditional compilation statements to avoid multiple inclusions of header files. Example 9-4 shows a header file that includes conditional compilation statements.

Example 9-4

```
//  Contents of myhead.h

#ifndef MYHEAD_H
#define MYHEAD_H

#define TRUE 1
#define FALSE 0
#define MAX_EMPS 100

#endif
```

In Example 9-4, the preprocessor interprets the `#ifndef` statement as follows:
If the symbolic constant MYHEAD_H is not defined then
  Define the symbolic constant MYHEAD_H
  Include the #define statements in the source code file.

When the preprocessor encounters additional `#include myhead.h` statements, the `#ifndef MYHEAD_H` statement will be false because MYHEAD_H will now be defined; as a result, the subsequent statements will not be included in the file. You might encounter this situation when compiling programs that contain multiple source code files. You also will run into this issue when you write object-oriented programs in C++.

Exercises

Exercise 9.10 ▶

M O D I F Y

The C++ program saved as Ch9-10.cpp in the Chapter9 folder on your Student Disk reads in mailing list data from a file named jewelry.dat and stores it in arrays of structures. The program then prints the mailing list data. Modify this program as follows (save all files in the Chapter9 folder):

  a. Put the structure templates and constants in a header file named jewel.h.
  b. Rewrite the program to call two functions, `read_data()` and `write_data()`.
  c. Store the `read_data()` function in a file named read_it.cpp.
  d. Store the `write_data()` function in a file named write_it.cpp.
  e. Store the main program in a file named Ch9-10a.cpp.

Be sure to use conditional compilation statements in your header file so you can include them in all of your .cpp files.

Exercise 9.11 ▶

D E B U G

You have modified the C++ program described in Exercise 8-12 so that you can store it in multiple files. The modified program is saved in the following files in the Chapter9 folder on your Student Disk:

bball.h	Structure template and constants
Ch9-11.cpp	Main program
read_in.cpp	`read_in()` function
print_report.cpp	`print_report()` function
sort_list.cpp	`sort_list()` function

This program is not compiling, however, so you do not know whether it works correctly. Find and fix the errors, and then save your corrected files in the Chapter9 folder using your own unique filenames.

Exercise 9.12 ▶

D E V E L O P

Write a C++ program for a garden shop that calls three functions. The first function should read the names of flowers and the quantity on hand for each variety. Store these data in an array of structures. The second function should alphabetize the list based on the flower name. The third function should print the contents of the array of structures (flower name and quantity on hand) in an attractive format. Organize your program in at least three separate files and create a header file for this application. You can use the file named flowers.dat (which is saved in the Chapter9 folder on your Student Disk) as an input file for your application. Save your program in the Chapter9 folder on your Student Disk using appropriate filenames.

S U M M A R Y

■ The preprocessor changes and adds to your source code files before the C++ compiler processes them.

■ Lines beginning with the pound sign (#) are preprocessor directives. Preprocessor directives are not C++ statements.

■ The `#define` directive is used to create symbolic constants.

■ The #define directive also is used to create macros. A macro is a small set of statements that can accept arguments.

■ Although macros and functions are similar, there are some differences between the two. Macros execute more rapidly than functions but can result in larger executable programs.

■ You should use the #include preprocessor directive to instruct the preprocessor to include a copy of a header file in your source code file.

■ You should use the #if, #ifdef, #ifndef, and #endif preprocessor directives to allow C++ to conditionally add lines to your source code files. This is referred to as conditional compilation.

PROGRESSIVE PROJECTS

1. Books and More

In Chapter 8, you modified the inventory control system program so that you could store the inventory data in an array of structures. In this assignment, you will "clean up" your application by organizing your functions and placing them in separate files. Create a header file for the application that includes the structure templates, constants, function declarations, macros, and other header files. When you are finished, compile the multiple .cpp files according to the directions for the specific compiler you are using. Save your program as Ch9-pp1 in the Chapter9 folder on your Student Disk. Give the individual files meaningful names. In the next chapter, you will change the way you store the inventory data again.

2. Baseball Simulation

In Chapter 8, you modified your baseball simulation program so that it stores the names and positions of players in an array of structures. In this assignment, you will "clean up" your program by organizing your functions and placing them in separate files. Create a header file for the application that includes the structure templates, constants, function declarations, macros, and other header files. When you are finished, compile the multiple .cpp files according to the directions for the specific compiler you are using. Save your program as Ch9-pp2 in the Chapter9 folder on your Student Disk. Give the individual files meaningful names. In the next chapter, you will change the way you store the player roster data again.

INDEPENDENT PROJECTS

1. States and Capitals Guessing Game

Write a C++ program to create a states and capitals guessing game. Your program should read in the state and capital data from a file named statecap.dat, which is saved in the Chapter9 folder on your Student Disk. A function in your program should generate a random number between 1 and 50. Your program should use this number to represent one of the 50 U.S. states and then display the name of that state. The user will guess the capital of that state. Another function in your program should get the user's answer and check to see whether it is correct. Yet another function should print the player's score, including both the total number of correct and incorrect guesses. The program should run until the user wants to quit.

Use good organization techniques to develop this program. For example, store your functions in separate files and create a header file for this application that includes structure templates, constants, function declarations, macros, and other header files. When you are finished, compile the multiple .cpp files according to the directions for the specific compiler you are using. Save your program as Ch9-ip1 in the Chapter9 folder on your Student Disk. Give the individual files meaningful names.

2. Restaurant Selector

Write a C++ program that provides the user with a list of restaurants, depending on the user's input. The program should read the data about restaurants from the file named food.dat in the Chapter9 folder on your Student Disk. The data file contains the following information for each restaurant: name, address, average meal cost, and food type. Your program should generate the restaurant list based on the user's input of a food type and/or dollar amount. The program should then print the appropriate restaurant data based on whether the average cost is less than a certain dollar amount, what type of food is served, or whether a specific type of food is served and the average cost is less than a certain dollar amount.

Use good organizational techniques to develop this program. For example, store your functions in separate files and create a header file for this application that includes structure templates, constants, function declarations, macros, and other header files. When you are finished, compile the multiple .cpp files according to the directions for the specific compiler you are using. Save your program as Ch9-ip2 in the Chapter9 folder on your Student Disk. Give the individual files meaningful names.

Introduction to Data Structures

Introduction ▶ In this chapter, you will review the use of the following data structures: singly linked lists, stacks, and queues.

A **data structure** is a way of organizing data. Understanding data structures is necessary to develop efficient programs. That is, the efficiency of a program is directly linked to the structure of the data being processed in the program. The data structure that you use might impact any or all of the following:

- The run-time efficiency of a program
- The efficiency of a program's use of system resources, such as RAM and disk storage
- A program's development cost

By studying data structures, you will learn more about existing, proven techniques used to design efficient programs. This knowledge will, in turn, help you to become a better C++ programmer.

Each of the data structures described in this chapter can be implemented in more than one way. You will review the techniques used to implement these data structures with pointers and dynamic memory allocation.

Dynamic Memory Allocation

One benefit of implementing data structures using pointers and dynamic memory allocation is that the data structure's size can increase or decrease as a program executes. Thus, rather than specifying the amount of memory that will be required when you write the program, you can dynamically ask for memory at execution time when it is needed by using the new operator. When the program no longer needs the dynamically allocated memory, you can release it using the delete operator.

Memory that is allocated dynamically is reserved in an area of memory called the **heap** or the **free store**. The new operator reserves storage on the heap, and the delete operator returns it to the heap.

The new operator either allocates enough memory on the heap for the data type you specify or allocates memory and then provides an initial value. In addition, you can dynamically allocate arrays with the new operator by using square brackets after the data type of the array and specifying the array's size. The value of the expression, which uses the new operator, is the memory address on the heap where the memory was allocated. This memory address is then assigned to a pointer variable, which you can use to access the dynamically allocated memory.

The delete operator returns dynamically allocated memory to the heap. You use the variable's address on the heap, which you stored in a pointer variable, with the delete operator. The delete operator deletes the item to which the pointer variable points, but it does not delete the pointer variable itself. Example 10-1 illustrates the use of the new and delete operators.

Syntax

▶ new data_type;
  new data_type(initial_value);
  new data_type[int expression];

Syntax

▶ delete pointer;
  delete []pointer;

Example 10-1

```cpp
int* int_ptr1;
int* int_ptr2;
double* dbl_ptr;
char* chr_ptr;
// Allocates enough memory to store an int.
// Heap address is now stored in int_ptr1.
int_ptr1 = new int;
// Allocates enough memory to store a double.
// Heap address is now stored in dbl_ptr.
dbl_ptr = new double;
// The value 10 is now stored on the heap.
*int_ptr1 = 10;
cout << *int_ptr1;  // Prints 10
// The value 22.50 is now stored on the heap.
*dbl_ptr = 22.50;
cout << *dbl_ptr;  // Prints 22.50
// Allocates and initializes enough memory to store
// an int; heap address is stored in int_ptr2.
int_ptr2 = new int(44);
cout << *int_ptr2;  // Prints 44
// Allocates 256 bytes on the heap.
// Beginning address is stored in chr_ptr.
chr_ptr = new char[256];
// Hello world is copied to the heap.
strcpy(chr_ptr, "Hello world");
cout << chr_ptr;  // Prints Hello world.
```

```
// Returns an integer's size of memory to the heap.
delete int_ptr1;
// Returns an integer's size of memory to the heap.
delete int_ptr2;
// Returns a double's size of memory to the heap.
delete dbl_ptr;
// Returns 256 bytes of memory to the heap.
delete []chr_ptr;
```

You also can use the new operator to allocate heap memory for a structure and the delete operator to return the memory used for the structure when it is no longer needed, as shown in Example 10-2.

Example 10-2

```
// Template for a structure with an integer member
// and a pointer member.
struct node
{
  int value;
  struct node* next;
};
// Declares a variable of type pointer to node structure.
struct node* newnode;
// Allocates enough memory on the heap to store a
// node structure; heap address is now stored in newnode.
newnode = new node;
// 10 is now stored on the heap in the value
// member of the structure pointed to by newnode.
newnode->value = 10;
cout << newnode->value;  // Prints 10
// Returns a node structure's amount of memory to the heap.
delete newnode;
```

When you use the new operator, the value of the expression in which it is used is the heap address where the memory was allocated; it is NULL if the heap space is sufficient to accomplish the memory allocation. Remember to test the allocation to ensure that it was successful in your program to avoid run-time errors. Example 10-3 shows how to perform this test.

Example 10-3

```
struct node
{
  int value;
  struct node* next;
};
struct node* newnode;
newnode = new node;
if(newnode == NULL)  // Allocation failed.
{
  cout << "Out of heap space."
  exit(1);
}
// Rest of program.
```

Linked List

A **linked list** is a data structure that minimizes the amount of data movement needed to insert data into and delete data from an ordered list. Each element in a linked list is called a **node**. A node contains both the data to be stored and a pointer to another node in the list.

Singly Linked List

In a **singly linked list**, each node contains data and a pointer. The pointer points to the next node in the list. Another pointer, called the **head pointer**, points to the first node in the list. The pointer stored in the last node of a singly linked list points to NULL, which represents the end of the list. Figure 10-1 shows a singly linked list that contains five nodes arranged in numerical order.

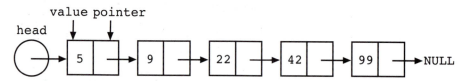

Figure 10-1: A singly linked list

You can create a singly linked list in C++ by using parallel arrays or dynamically allocated structures and pointer variables. In this book, you will use the latter implementation.

Creating a Singly Linked List

To create a singly linked list, you must create a structure template that is used to create the nodes in your list and a pointer variable that is used as the head pointer so you can point to the beginning of your list. Initially, the linked list should be empty—you assign NULL to the head pointer to create an empty list. Example 10-4 illustrates the C++ code that creates an empty linked list.

Example 10-4

```
struct node
{
  int value;
  struct node* next;
};

// Pointer used to point to the first node in the list.
struct node* head;
head = NULL;  // Creates an empty list.
```

Figure 10-2 shows the empty list created by the code shown in Example 10-4.

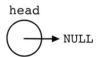

Figure 10-2: An empty singly linked list

Inserting Nodes

After you create an empty singly linked list, you can insert nodes into this list by dynamically allocating storage for the new node and then finding the proper location in the list to insert it. To dynamically allocate the new node, you use the new operator. You then use two pointers, named `current` and `previous`, to insert the nodes. To find the proper location to insert the node, you compare the value stored in the new node that you want to insert with the value stored in the node pointed to by the `current` pointer. The `previous` pointer always points to the previous node in the list. You keep moving the `current` and `previous` pointers through the list until you find the desired insertion point. You then insert the new node between the nodes pointed to by the `current` and `previous` pointers. This process is accomplished with assignment statements that make the node pointed to by the `previous` pointer point to the new node and then making the new node point to the node that `current` is pointing to. Example 10-5 shows the code to accomplish the insertion by modifying pointer values.

Example 10-5

```
cin >> number;
newnode = new node;
if(newnode == NULL)
{
  cout << "Out of heap space." << endl;
  exit(1);
}
newnode->value = number;
previous->next = newnode;
newnode->next = current;
```

Figure 10-3a illustrates a dynamically allocated node, and Figure 10-3b shows how pointers are modified when you insert a node with a value of 35 in a singly linked list.

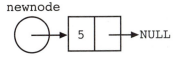

Figure 10-3a: Allocation of a node

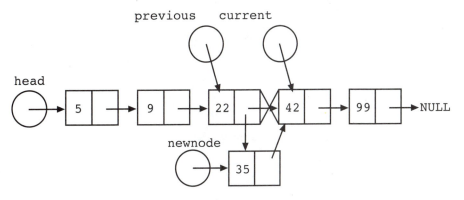

Figure 10-3b: Inserting a new node in a singly linked list

You must account for two special cases when inserting a node into a singly linked list: inserting a node in an empty list, and inserting a node before the first node in the list.

A singly linked list is empty when `head == NULL`. You can perform a simple test to see whether this condition is true. If you are inserting a node into an empty list, you will need to change the value of the `head` pointer. Example 10-6 shows the code that inserts a node into an empty list.

Example 10-6

```
if(head == NULL)
{
  newnode->next = NULL;
  head = newnode;
}
```

Figure 10-4 illustrates the insertion of a node into an empty singly linked list.

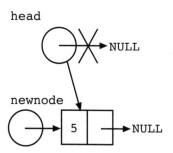

Figure 10-4: Inserting into an empty list

When you need to insert a node before the first node in a singly linked list, you should test to see whether the data in `newnode` is less than the data stored in the node pointed to by the `head` pointer. Example 10-7 shows the code to accomplish this test.

Example 10-7

```
if(newnode->value < head->value)
{
  newnode->next = head;
  head = newnode;
}
```

Figure 10-5 illustrates the insertion of a node before the first node in a singly linked list.

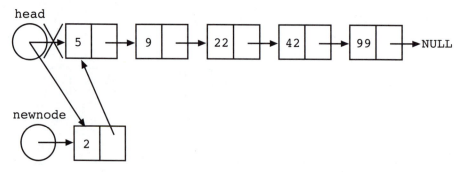

Figure 10-5: Inserting a node before the first node in a singly linked list

Example 10-8 uses an algorithm coded in C++ that allows you to insert a node into a singly linked list and take these special cases into consideration. In this algorithm, the `insert()` function receives a pointer to a pointer to a node structure, allowing the `insert()` function to change the value of the head pointer.

Example 10-8

```
const int TRUE = 1;
const int FALSE = 0;
void insert(struct node ** hd, int item)
{
  struct node* current, *previous, *newnode;
  int found;

  if(*hd == NULL)  // List is empty.
  {
    newnode = new node;   // Allocate memory.
    if(newnode == NULL)
    {
      cout << "Out of heap space." << endl;
      exit(1);
    }
    newnode->value = item; // Store item in newnode
    // newnode's next pointer should point to NULL.
    newnode->next = NULL;
    // head pointer now points to newnode.
    *head = newnode;
  }
  // item comes before first node in the list.
  else if(item < (*hd)->value)
  {
    newnode = new node;   // Allocate memory.
    if(newnode == NULL)
    {
      cout << "Out of heap space." << endl;
      exit(1);
    }
    newnode->value = item; // Store item in newnode.
    newnode->next = *hd;  // newnode points to head.
    // head pointer now points to newnode.
    *hd = newnode;
  }
  else  // General case, find a place for the item.
  {
    newnode = new node;   // Allocate memory
    if(newnode == NULL)
    {
      cout << "Out of heap space." << endl;
      exit(1);
    }
    newnode->value = item; // Store item in newnode.
    // previous pointer starts at head of list.
    previous = *hd;
    // current points to second node in list.
    current = (*hd)->next;
    found = FALSE;
    // Search list for insertion point.
    while(current != NULL && found == FALSE)
    {
      // As long as this is true, keep looking for
      // insertion point.
      if(item > current->value)
```

```
      {
        // previous now points to next node.
        previous = current;
        // current now points to next node.
        current = current->next;
      }
      else
      // When item is < current's value then
      // insertion point is found.
      found = TRUE;
    }
    // Modify pointers to accomplish the insertion.
    newnode->next = current;
    previous->next = newnode;
  }
  return;
}
```

Figure 10-6 illustrates a pointer to a pointer, which is sometimes called a **double indirection**. The address of the variable named `head` is passed to the function. As the variable `head` is a pointer, you are actually passing an address indicating where an address is stored in memory. In the `insert()` function, the address of the `head` pointer is stored in the argument named `hd`. Therefore, you must declare `hd` as a pointer to a pointer to a node structure because it contains an address specifying where another address is stored.

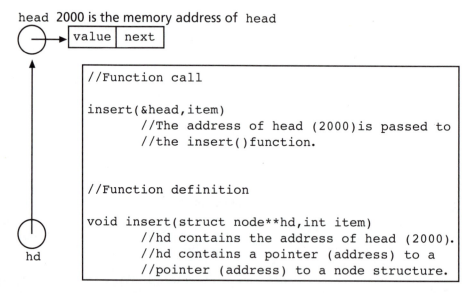

Figure 10-6: Double indirection

Traversing a Singly Linked List

To print or search the contents of a singly linked list, you begin at the head of the list and follow the next pointer to the next node in the list until you reach the NULL pointer. The NULL pointer marks the end of the list.

Example 10-9 shows an algorithm coded in C++ that traverses a singly linked list and prints the data items stored in the list.

Example 10-9

```
void traverse(struct node* hd)
{
  struct node* current;

  current = hd;  // Start at beginning of list.

  // Stay in loop until you reach end of list.
  while(current != NULL)
  {
    cout << current->value << endl;
    current = current->next;  // Point to next node.
  }
  return;
}
```

Deleting Nodes

To delete a node from a singly linked list, you modify the pointers; therefore, no data movement is necessary. First, you search the list for the item to be deleted by using two pointers, current and previous. When you find the node, the current pointer will point to the node that contains the item to be deleted; the previous pointer will point to the previous node in the list. Figure 10-7 shows the changes made to these pointers to accomplish the deletion of the node with the value 22 from a singly linked list. The next pointer of the node pointed to by the previous pointer is modified so that it points to the node that is pointed to by the next pointer of the node pointed to by the current pointer. As you can see in Figure 10-7, the node to which the current pointer points is no longer part of the singly linked list.

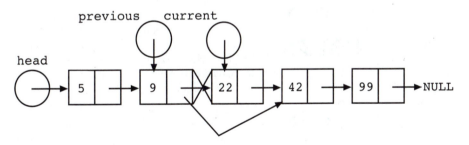

Figure 10-7: Deleting a node from a singly linked list

Example 10-10 shows an algorithm coded in C++ that deletes a node from a singly linked list.

Example 10-10

```
void delete_node(struct node** hd, int item)
{
  struct node* temp, *previous, *current;

  // Delete first node in list.
  if(item == (*hd)->value)
  {
    temp = *hd;         // Save value of head pointer.
    *hd = (*hd)->next;  // Change value of head pointer.

    delete (temp);  // Release the deleted node's memory.
  }
```

```
    else
    {
      // previous points to first node in list.
      previous = *hd;
      // current points to second node in list.
      current = (*hd)->next;
      // Search for the item.
      while(current->value != item && current != NULL)
      {
        current = current->next;   // Point to next node.
        previous = previous->next; // Point to next node.
      }
      if(current != NULL)
      {
        // Modify pointer at deletion point.
        temp = current;
        previous->next = current->next;
        delete (temp); // Release memory
      }
      else
        cout << "Item not found in list." << endl;

    }
    return;
}
```

Exercises

Exercise 10.1 ▶

M O D I F Y

The C++ program saved as Ch10-1.cpp in the Chapter10 folder on your Student Disk calculates raises for the employees of the XYZ Candy Company. Modify this program so that it stores the employees' names, salaries, and years of service in a linked list instead of parallel arrays. Save your modified program as Ch10-1a.cpp in the Chapter10 folder. The input file for this program, candy.dat, is saved in the Chapter10 folder.

Exercise 10.2 ▶

D E B U G

The C++ program saved as Ch10-2.cpp in the Chapter10 folder on your Student Disk reads words from a file named test.dat. The words need to be stored in an alphabetically ordered list along with the number of times that each word appears in the file. The program does not work correctly because it does not handle duplicates appropriately. Find and fix the errors, and then save your corrected program as Ch10-2a.cpp in the Chapter10 folder.

Exercise 10.3 ▶

D E V E L O P

Authorized shareholders of your company are allowed to attend a stockholders' meeting. Write a program that reads a list of shareholders who attended last year's meeting into a singly linked list. These input data need to be ordered alphabetically by last name and then by first name. The input file containing the list of shareholders is saved as share.dat in the Chapter10 folder on your Student Disk. After your program reads in last year's attendees, it should allow the list to be updated with additions and deletions needed for this year's meeting. The program should make the following updates:

Add These Names	Delete These Names
Fred Founder	William Paca
Bob Begine	William Whipple
Sam Starter	

After the program updates the list, print the new list of shareholders in alphabetical order by last name and then by first name. Save your finished program as Ch10-3a.cpp in the Chapter10 folder.

Stack

A **stack** is a special kind of list that is sometimes called a **LIFO list** (Last In, First Out). When using a stack in a C++ program, all insertions and deletions occur at one end of the list, known as the top of the stack. Inserting into the stack is called "pushing onto the stack," and deleting a node from a stack is referred to as "popping the stack."

A compiler might use a stack to remember the location to which a program should return when a subroutine or function finishes executing. Figure 10-8 illustrates the use of a stack for this purpose.

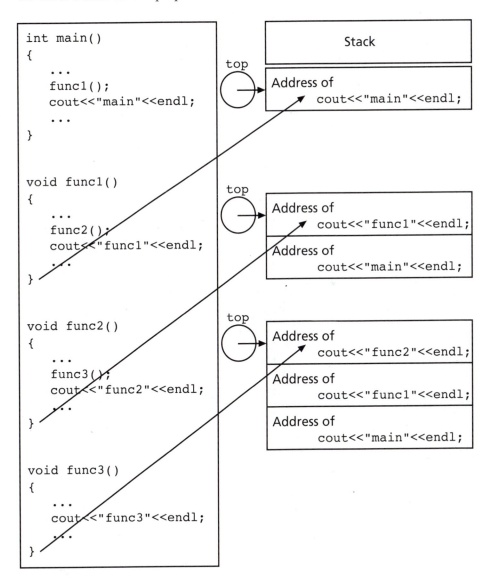

Figure 10-8: Using a stack for function calls

Calculators that use Reverse Polish notation also might use a stack, as shown in Figure 10-9.

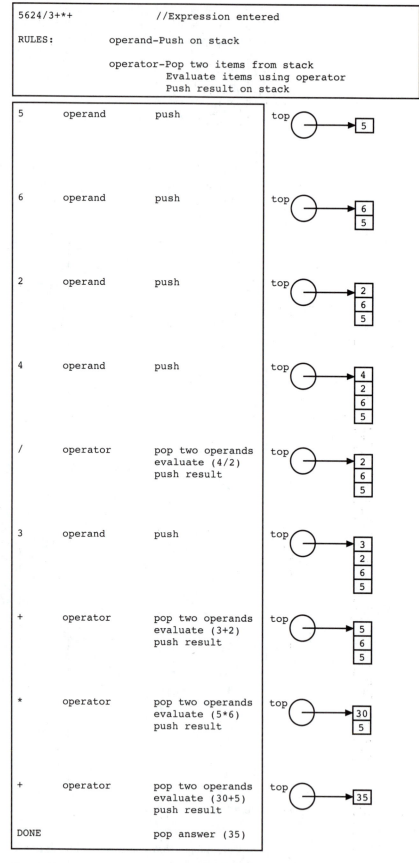

Figure 10-9: Using a stack for a Reverse Polish calculator

Creating a Stack

To create a stack, you must create a structure template that will be used to dynamically allocate nodes that will, in turn, be pushed onto or popped from the stack. In addition, you must declare a pointer variable that points to the node on the top of the stack, as shown in Example 10-11. Assigning NULL to the top pointer creates an empty stack.

Example 10-11

```
const int MAX_MESSAGE = 256;
struct node
{
  char message[MAX_MESSAGE];
  struct node* next;
};

// Pointer that will point
// to the top of the stack.
struct node* top;

top = NULL;  // Creates an empty stack.
```

Figure 10-10 illustrates an empty stack.

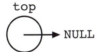

Figure 10-10: Empty stack

Pushing onto the Stack

All new nodes are pushed onto the stack at the location pointed to by the pointer variable named top. When you push a new node onto the stack, the value of the top pointer changes so that it points to the newly added node. Figure 10-11 illustrates how a stack changes as nodes are pushed onto it.

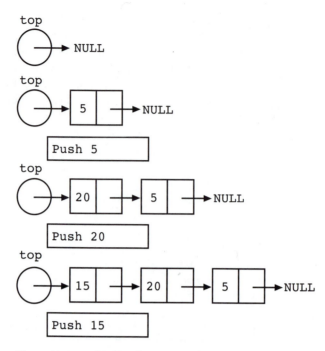

Figure 10-11: Pushing nodes onto a stack

Example 10-12 shows an algorithm for pushing a node onto a stack.

Example 10-12

```
void push(struct node** top)
{
  struct node* newnode;

  newnode = new node;  // Allocate memory.
  if(newnode == NULL)  // Not able to allocate memory.
  {
    cout << "Out of stack space." << endl;
    exit(1);
  }

  // Get message from user.
  cout << "Enter your message:";
  cin.getline(newnode->msg,MAX_MESSAGE);
  // newnode now points to top of stack.
  newnode->next = *top;
  // top pointer now points to new node.
  *top = newnode;
  return;

}
```

Popping the Stack

To delete a node from a stack, the node pointed to by the top pointer is popped from the stack. The top pointer is adjusted so that it points to the node that is pointed to by the next pointer in the node currently pointed to by the top pointer. Figure 10-12 illustrates how a stack changes as nodes are popped from it.

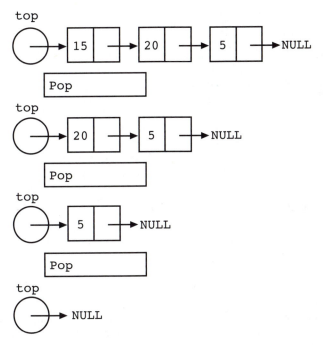

Figure 10-12: Popping nodes from a stack

Example 10-13 shows an algorithm that pops a node from a stack.

Example 10-13

```
void pop(struct node** top, char return_msg[])
{
  struct node* temp_ptr;

  if(*top == NULL)  // Can't pop an empty stack.
  {
    cout << "Stack is empty." << endl;
    strcpy(return_msg, "");
  }
  else
  {
    // Copy message from top of stack.
    strcpy(return_msg, (*top)->msg);
    // Save value of next node on the stack.
    temp_ptr = (*top)->next;
    // Free memory allocated for node pointed to by top.
    delete *top;
    // Change top pointer's value.
    *top = temp_ptr;
  }

  return;
}
```

Exercises

Exercise 10.4 ▶

The command editor for the MegaSwift Operating System uses the # character as the kill character. For example, if a user types the command `lisy#t myg#fio#le`, the command editor interprets it as `list myfile`. Add functionality to this command editor so that it will interpret the @ character as the line kill character. For example, if a user types the command `Listttt myfeiii@`, the command interpreter should interpret the input as killing the entire line, allowing the user to begin again. Alter the C++ program saved as Ch10-4.cpp in the Chapter10 folder on your Student Disk to make this change, and then save your modified program as Ch10-4a.cpp.

Exercise 10.5 ▶

The program saved as Ch10-5.cpp in the Chapter10 folder on your Student Disk implements the Reverse Polish calculator mentioned earlier in this chapter. This implementation of the calculator deals with single-digit input values only. For example, the expression `96 + 5 *` is interpreted as `(9 + 6) * 5`, and not as `96 + 5`. The current program does not work correctly. Find and fix the errors and then save the modified program as Ch10-5a.cpp in the Chapter10 folder.

Exercise 10.6 ▶

Write a program that asks a user to input a base-10 number and convert it to a binary number. The algorithm for accomplishing this processing appears in pseudocode below.

Step 1: Assign the decimal value to a variable named number
Step 2: Divide number by 2 and save the quotient in a variable
     named qtnt and the remainder in a variable named rmndr
Step 3: rmndr is the next binary digit
Step 4: if qtnt is equal to 0
     all binary digits have been processed
     else
     assign qtnt to number
Step 5: Repeat beginning with Step 2

Save your program as Ch10-6a.cpp in the Chapter10 folder.

Queue

Like a stack, a **queue** is a special kind of list that is sometimes called a **FIFO list** (First In, First Out). When you use a queue in a C++ program, all insertions take place at one end of the queue, called the **rear**. All deletions occur at the other end of the queue, called the **front**. Two pointers, named `front` and `rear`, are maintained to allow for the insertion and deletion of nodes in a queue.

You already are familiar with queues. A checkout line at the supermarket or a waiting line at the bank is a queue, as is the line of cars at a tollbooth. Computer processes waiting to be executed by the CPU also might be a queue.

Creating a Queue

To create a queue, you create a structure template that will be used to dynamically allocate nodes for the queue. You must also declare two pointer variables, `front` and `rear`, that point to the first and last nodes in the queue, respectively. Assigning

NULL to both the `front` and `rear` pointers creates an empty queue. Example 10-14 shows the C++ code for creating an empty queue.

Example 10-14

```
const int MAX_NAME = 30;
struct node
{
  char name[MAX_NAME];
  struct node* next;
};

// Pointers used to point to insertion and
// deletion point in a queue.
struct node* front, *rear;

// Creates an empty queue.
front = NULL;
rear = NULL;
```

Figure 10-13 illustrates an empty queue.

Figure 10-13: An empty queue

Adding a Node to a Queue

All new nodes are added to a queue at the location pointed to by the `rear` pointer variable. After adding a node, the value of the `rear` pointer changes so that it points to the most recently added node. Figure 10-14 illustrates the addition of a node to a queue.

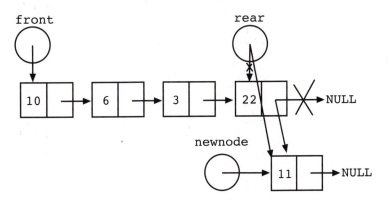

Figure 10-14: Adding a node to a queue

Example 10-15 shows an algorithm for adding a node to a queue.

Example 10-15

```cpp
const int NAME_LEN = 30;
void put(struct node** front, struct node** rear)
{
  struct node* newnode;

  newnode = new node;      // Allocate memory.
  if(newnode == NULL)      // Out of heap space.
  {
    cout << "Out of heap space." << endl;
    exit(1);
  }

  cout << "Enter a name:" ;   // Get user input
  cin.getline(newnode->name,NAME_LEN);
  // At end of queue, newnode always points to NULL.
  newnode->next = NULL;
  if(*front == NULL)  // Empty queue
  {
    // Both front and rear point to newnode.
    *front = newnode;
    *rear = newnode;
  }
  else
  {

    // The next pointer of the node to which rear is
    // pointing now points to the new node.
    (*rear)->next = newnode;
    // rear now points to newnode.
    *rear = newnode;
  }

  return;
}
```

Deleting a Node from a Queue

To delete a node from a queue, the node pointed to by the `front` pointer is removed by adjusting pointers. The value of the `front` pointer changes so that it points to the node pointed to by the `front` pointer's next pointer. Figure 10-15 shows the node with a value of 10 deleted from a queue.

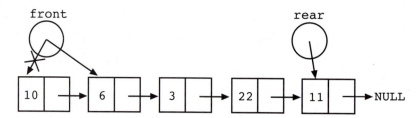

Figure 10-15: Deleting a node from a queue

Example 10-16 shows an algorithm for deleting a node from a queue.

Example 10-16

```
void get(struct node** front, char return_msg[]
{
  struct node* temp_ptr;

  // Can't delete from an empty queue.
  if(*front == NULL)
  {
    cout << "Queue is empty." << endl;
    strcpy(return_msg, "");
  }
  else
  {
    // Copy name from front of queue.
    strcpy(return_msg, (*front)->name);
    // Saves value of front pointer.
    temp_ptr = *front;
    // front pointer now points to second node in queue.
    *front = temp_ptr->next;
    delete temp_ptr;  // Free memory allocated
  }

  return;
}
```

Exercises

Exercise 10.7 ▶

M O D I F Y

The program saved as Ch10-7.cpp in the Chapter10 folder on your Student Disk manages a list of customers who are waiting for Chicago Bulls tickets. The program allows a clerk to add and delete customers from the waiting list and to print a list of every customer on the list. This list is managed as a queue. Modify this program so that it does not allow duplicate records in the queue. A duplicate is defined as a record with the same Social Security number as a record already in the queue. Save your modified program as Ch10-7a.cpp in the Chapter10 folder.

Exercise 10.8 ▶

D E B U G

Charles Carr, the owner of Carr's Motor Sales, has asked you to write a C++ program that manages a list of customers who are on a waiting list for car models that are not currently in stock. Your program, which is saved as Ch10-8.cpp in the Chapter10 folder on your Student Disk, compiles but does not produce the correct results. You used a queue to store each customer's name and other pertinent information about that customer. When you print the contents of the queue, it seems to miss what should be the first name in the waiting list. Find and fix the error, and then save the corrected program as Ch10-8a.cpp in the Chapter10 folder.

Exercise 10.9 ▶

D E V E L O P

Write a C++ program that simulates an operating system's management of processes that are submitted for execution on the CPU. Processes should be placed in a queue and executed on a first-come, first-served basis. Your program should open an input file named batch.dat, found in the Chapter10 folder on your Student Disk. Each line of the batch.dat file contains one of the following commands:

Command	Description
Add	Adds a process to the queue and assigns a job number
Delete	Deletes a process from the queue
Status	Lists all processes currently in the queue

When you are finished, save your program as Ch10-9a.cpp in the Chapter10 folder.

S U M M A R Y

- A data structure is a way of organizing data.

- The efficiency of a program often depends on the type of data structure used.

- One method used to implement data structures employs pointers and dynamically allocated nodes to store data.

- You can use the `new` operator to allocate memory dynamically. You can use the `delete` operator to return dynamically allocated memory.

- A linked list is a data structure that minimizes the amount of data movement needed to insert data into and delete data from a list.

- A singly linked list consists of dynamically allocated nodes that contain data and a pointer to the next node in the list. The `head` pointer points to the beginning of the list. The last node in a singly linked list points to `NULL`.

- Algorithms exist for inserting a node into a singly linked list, deleting a node from a singly linked list, and traversing a singly linked list.

- A stack is a special kind of linked list that is sometimes called a LIFO list (Last In, First Out).

- All insertions (push) and deletions (pop) occur at one end of the stack, referred to as the top of the stack.

- Algorithms exist for pushing nodes onto a stack and popping nodes off a stack.

- A queue is a special kind of linked list that is sometimes called a FIFO list (First In, First Out).

- All insertions into a queue occur at one end of the queue, called the rear. All deletions occur at the other end of the queue, called the front.

- Algorithms exist for adding nodes to the rear of a queue and deleting nodes from the front of a queue.

P R O G R E S S I V E   P R O J E C T S

1. Books and More

In Chapter 9, you modified the Books and More inventory control system so that it was stored in multiple files. You also created a header file for the application. In this assignment, you will change the storage method so that the inventory data are placed in a singly linked list. Order the list alphabetically, based on each book's title. Save your program as Ch10-pp1.cpp in the Chapter10 folder on your Student Disk.

2. Baseball Simulation

In Chapter 9, you modified the baseball simulation program so that it was stored in multiple files. You also created a header file for the application. In this assignment, you will change the method for storing the player rosters so that the players' names and their positions are placed in a singly linked list. Order the list based on position in the batting order. A batting order number has been added to the files named team1.dat and team2.dat in the Chapter10 folder on your Student Disk. This new implementation of the roster will allow you to make substitutions easily as the game progresses. Save your program as Ch10-pp2.cpp in the Chapter10 folder.

INDEPENDENT PROJECTS

1. Compiler Functionality

One function of a C++ compiler is ensuring that the numbers of opening and closing curly braces and opening and closing parentheses match. Write a C++ program that reads a C++ source code file and determines whether the numbers of opening and closing curly braces and opening and closing parentheses match. You can envision this program as being a very small part of a compiler. Use any of your C++ source code files as input. Generate meaningful compiler errors. Include a stack in your implementation of this program. Save your program as Ch10-ip1.cpp in the Chapter10 folder on your Student Disk.

2. Concert Tickets

You are managing ticket sales for three upcoming concerts. All three concerts are sold out, but you are adding the names of customers who still want tickets to a waiting list. Add the following names to the waiting list for a particular concert, along with the number of tickets each customer wants to purchase. You might want to use more than one queue to accomplish this process.

Customer Name	Number of Tickets Needed	Concert
Fred First	5	Bruce Springsteen
May Munro	4	Jimmy Dale Gilmore
Helen Howard	2	Bruce Springsteen
Barry Burke	4	Lyle Lovett
Gary Gower	3	Jimmy Dale Gilmore
Tom Tilton	1	Lyle Lovett
Will West	2	Bruce Springsteen

After adding these customers' names to the list, process the following returns, and then determine who gets the tickets. Reduce the number of tickets for which a customer is waiting, if appropriate.

Customer Name	Number of Tickets Returned	Concert
John Jacobs	6	Bruce Springsteen
Steve Shelton	2	Jimmy Dale Gilmore
Paul Peters	4	Lyle Lovett

APPENDIX A

C++ Keywords

and	double	not_eq	this
and_eq	dynamiccast	operator	throw
asm	else	or	true
auto	enum	or_eq	try
bitand	explicit	overload	typedef
bitor	extern	private	typeid
bool	false	protected	typename
break	float	public	uchar_t
case	for	register	union
catch	friend	reinterpret_cast	unsigned
char	goto	return	using
class	if	short	virtual
compl	inline	signed	void
const	int	sizeof	volatile
constcast	long	state_cast	wchar_t
continue	mutable	static	while
default	namespace	struct	xor
delete	new	switch	xor_eq
do	not	template	

Figure A-1: C++ Keywords

ASCII Collating Sequence

Symbol	Meaning	ASCII in Decimal Representation	ASCII in Binary Representation	ASCII in Hex Representation
.	Null	0	0000 0000	0
SOH	Start of header	1	0000 0001	1
STX	Start of text	2	0000 0010	2
ETX	End of text	3	0000 0011	3
EOT	End of transmission	4	0000 0100	4
ENQ	Enquiry	5	0000 0101	5
ACK	Acknowledge	6	0000 0110	6
BEL	Bell (beep)	7	0000 0111	7
BS	Back space	8	0000 1000	8
HT	Horizontal tab	9	0000 1001	9
LF	Line feed	10	0000 1010	A
VT	Vertical tab	11	0000 1011	B
FF	Form feed	12	0000 1100	C

Figure B-1: Standard ASCII Character Set

Symbol	Meaning	ASCII in Decimal Representation	ASCII in Binary Representation	ASCII in Hex Representation
CR	Carriage return	13	0000 1101	D
SO	Shift out	14	0000 1110	E
SI	Shift in	15	0000 1111	F
DLE	Data link escape	16	0001 0000	10
DC1	Device control one	17	0001 0001	11
DC2	Device control two	18	0001 0010	12
DC3	Device control three	19	0001 0011	13
DC4	Device control four	20	0001 0100	14
NAK	Negative acknowledge	21	0001 0101	15
SYN	Synchronous idle	22	0001 0110	16
ETB	End of transmitted block	23	0001 0111	17
CAN	Cancel	24	0001 1000	18
EM	End of medium	25	0001 1001	19
SUB	Substitute	26	0001 1010	1A
ESC	Escape	27	0001 1011	1B
FS	File separator	28	0001 1100	1C
GS	Group separator	29	0001 1101	1D
RS	Record separator	30	0001 1110	1E
US	Unit separator	31	0001 1111	1F
b/	Space	32	0010 0000	20
!	Exclamation point	33	0010 0001	21
"	Quotation mark	34	0010 0010	22
#	Number sign	35	0010 0011	23
$	Dollar sign	36	0010 0100	24
%	Percent sign	37	0010 0101	25
&	Ampersand	38	0010 0110	26
'	Apostrophe, prime sign	39	0010 0111	27

Figure B-1: Standard ASCII Character Set (continued)

Symbol	Meaning	ASCII in Decimal Representation	ASCII in Binary Representation	ASCII in Hex Representation
(	Opening parenthesis	40	0010 1000	28
)	Closing parenthesis	41	0010 1001	29
*	Asterisk	42	0010 1010	2A
+	Plus sign	43	0010 1011	2B
,	Comma	44	0010 1100	2C
-	Hyphen, Minus sign	45	0010 1101	2D
.	Period, Decimal point	46	0010 1110	2E
/	Forward slash	47	0010 1111	2F
0		48	0011 0000	30
1		49	0011 0001	31
2		50	0010 0010	32
3		51	0010 0011	33
4		52	0010 0100	34
5		53	0010 0101	35
6		54	0010 0110	36
7		55	0010 0111	37
8		56	0010 1000	38
9		57	0010 1001	39
:	Colon	58	0010 1010	3A
;	Semicolon	59	0010 1011	3B
<	Less than sign	60	0010 1100	3C
=	Equal sign	61	0010 1101	3D
>	Greater than sign	62	0011 1110	3E
?	Question mark	63	0011 1111	3F
@	Commercial at sign	64	0100 0000	40
A		65	0100 0001	41
B		66	0100 0010	42
C		67	0100 0011	43
D		68	0100 0100	44
E		69	0100 0101	45
F		70	0100 0110	46
G		71	0100 0111	47
H		72	0100 1000	48

Figure B-1: Standard ASCII Character Set (continued)

Symbol	Meaning	ASCII in Decimal Representation	ASCII in Binary Representation	ASCII in Hex Representation
I		73	0100 1001	49
J		74	0100 1010	4A
K		75	0100 1011	4B
L		76	0100 1100	4C
M		77	0100 1101	4D
N		78	0100 1110	4E
O		79	0100 1111	4F
P		80	0101 0000	50
Q		81	0101 0001	51
R		82	0101 0010	52
S		83	0101 0011	53
T		84	0101 0100	54
U		85	0101 0101	55
V		86	0101 0110	56
W		87	0101 0111	57
X		88	0101 1000	58
Y		89	0101 1001	59
Z		90	0101 1010	5A
[	Opening bracket	91	0101 1011	5B
\	Back slash	92	0101 1100	5C
]	Closing bracket	93	0101 1101	5D
^	Caret	94	0101 1110	5E
_	Underscore	95	0101 1111	5F
`	Grave accent	96	0110 0000	60
a		97	0110 0001	61
b		98	0110 0010	62
c		99	0110 0011	63
d		100	0110 0100	64
e		101	0110 0101	65
f		102	0110 0110	66
g		103	0110 0111	67
h		104	0110 1000	68
i		105	0110 1001	69
j		106	0110 1010	6A
k		107	0110 1011	6B
l		108	0110 1100	6C
m		109	0110 1101	6D
n		110	0110 1110	6E

Figure B-1: Standard ASCII Character Set (continued)

Symbol	Meaning	ASCII in Decimal Representation	ASCII in Binary Representation	ASCII in Hex Representation
o		111	0110 1111	6F
p		112	0111 0000	70
q		113	0111 0001	71
r		114	0111 0010	72
s		115	0111 0011	73
t		116	0111 0100	74
u		117	0111 0101	75
v		118	0111 0110	76
w		119	0111 0111	77
x		120	0111 1000	78
y		121	0111 1001	79
z		122	0111 1010	7A
{	Opening curly brace	123	0111 1011	7B
l	Split vertical bar	124	0111 1100	7C
}	Closing curly brace	125	0111 1101	7D
~	Tilde	126	0111 1110	7E
DEL	Delete	127	0111 1111	7F

Figure B-1: Standard ASCII Character Set (continued)

Index